COMPOSITION

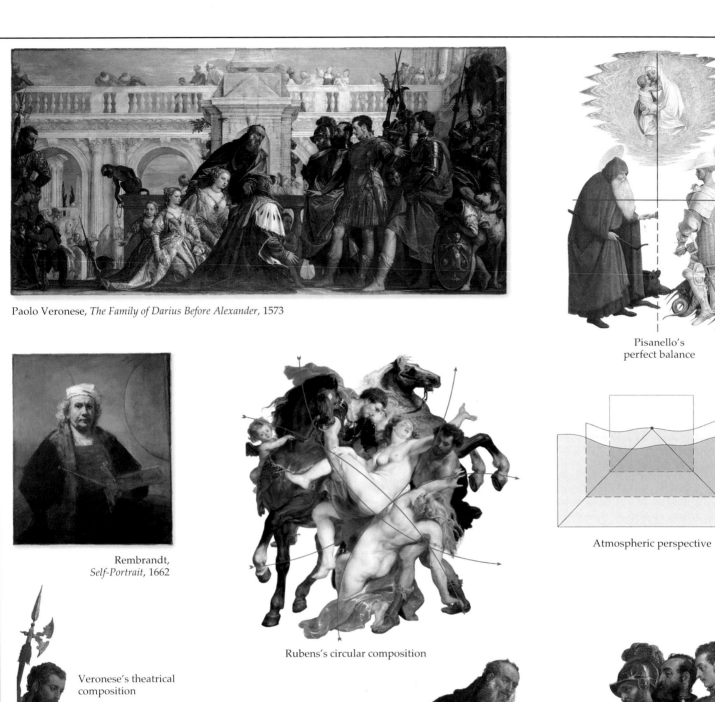

Paolo Veronese, *The Family of Darius Before Alexander*, 1573

Pisanello's
perfect balance

Rembrandt,
Self-Portrait, 1662

Rubens's circular composition

Atmospheric perspective

Veronese's theatrical
composition

EYEWITNESS ART

COMPOSITION

SARAH KENT

Nautilus shell with
Golden Ratio proportions

Jan Vermeer, *The Artist in his Studio*, 1665

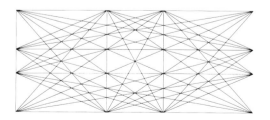

Dynamics of a Golden Section rectangle

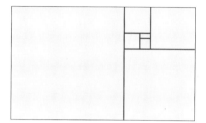

Division of a Golden Rectangle

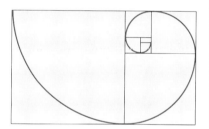

Golden Section spiral

Gwen John, *Nude Girl*, 1909–10

DORLING KINDERSLEY

LONDON • NEW YORK • STUTTGART

Pieter Bruegel the Elder,
Parable of the Blind, 1568

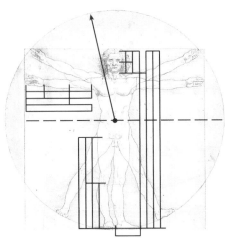

Leonardo da Vinci, *The Proportions
of the Human Figure*, 1492

Early camera

Raphael, *Madonna of the Chair*, 1514

A DORLING KINDERSLEY BOOK

Project editors Helen Castle, Phil Hunt
Art editor Mark Johnson Davies
Senior editor Gwen Edmonds
Senior art editor Claire Legemah
Managing editor Sean Moore
Managing art editor Toni Kay
Picture researchers Julia Harris-Voss, Jo Walton
DTP designer Zirrinia Austin
Production controller Meryl Silbert

This Eyewitness ®/™ Art book
first published in Great Britain in 1995 by
Dorling Kindersley Limited,
9 Henrietta Street, London WC2E 8PS

A CIP catalogue record for this book is
available from the British Library

ISBN 0 7513 1052 2

Colour reproduction by GRB Editrice s.r.l.
Printed in Italy by A. Mondadori Editore, Verona

Peter Paul Rubens,
Prometheus Bound, 1612

Photo taken by Edgar Degas

Hans Holbein the Younger,
Christ in the Tomb, 1521

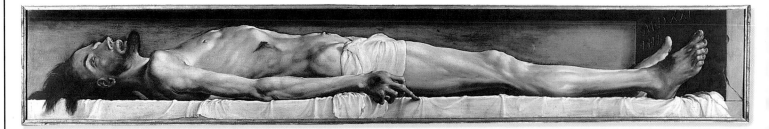

Contents

Meindert Hobbema, *The Avenue, Middelharnis*, 1689

Composing a picture

Hᴏᴡ ᴅᴏᴇꜱ ᴀɴ ᴀʀᴛɪꜱᴛ set about arranging the elements in a picture? Some painters would be unable to answer that question because they work intuitively, while others plan every detail in advance. Whether conscious or not, decisions are never arbitrary. Every ingredient – size and placement of figures, tone, colour, brushwork – alters the meaning of a picture. A person placed in the centre has more impact than someone tucked in a corner. A balanced composition affects us differently from a chaotic tangle. Edouard Manet (1832–83) used his favourite model, Victorine Meurent, in each of these paintings, but the compositions are very different from one another. The figures have been arranged to create a sense of intimacy or detachment, closeness or distance.

WOMAN PLAYING A GUITAR
Edouard Manet; 1867–68; 66 x 82 cm (26 x 32¼ in)
Manet's paintings of women were often quite radical. Traditionally, the emphasis had been on women looking charming, seductive, and idle. But Manet chose to paint working women – dancers, singers, and barmaids – as well as his leisured friends. Victorine Meurent was an artist who would later exhibit at the Paris Salon. She also played the guitar, and Manet places her with her back to us, absorbed in her music. To show a woman preoccupied in her own affairs is so unusual that one tends to see her as an allegorical figure – like the personification of history (pp. 32–33) – rather than as a person in her own right. Most portrait paintings are in a vertical format, but Manet selected a horizontal canvas for this depiction of Victorine, to allow him to emphasize her outstretched arm holding the guitar.

PORTRAIT OF VICTORINE MEURENT
Edouard Manet; 1862; 43 x 43 cm (17 x 17 in)
Manet was often criticized for painting in strong darks and lights with no half-tones in between. "It is preferable, even if it seems brutal," he insisted, "to pass brusquely from light to dark rather than to accumulate things the eye cannot see and which not only weaken the vigour of the lights but attenuate the coloration of the shadows." Manet puts Victorine in the spotlight to become a bright shape against a dark ground. He does not provide her with a context, such as a room, flowers, or other people. This isolation and her separation from the background also set her apart emotionally, so that one assumes her to be a loner. The harsh light hardens her features, giving her cheek and jaw a sharp outline that implies strength of character, while her severe hairstyle and unsmiling gaze confirm the idea that she is forceful and uncompromising.

The Railway

EDOUARD MANET *1873; 93 x 114 cm (36½ x 45 in)*
Manet paints Victorine in warm flesh tones to suggest diffuse outdoor light. Her loose hair and hat give her a "feminine" appearance. The composition is very unusual. Victorine and the girl form two separate verticals that are linked by the girl's arm. Victorine looks towards us while the girl turns away to watch the passing trains. They are the same height, but Victorine's dark dress gives her a weightier presence that anchors the picture. The right side of the picture is empty, save for the railings, the steam, and a bunch of grapes.

DÉJEUNER SUR L'HERBE
Edouard Manet; 1863; 208 x 264 cm (6 ft 9 in x 8 ft 8 in)
Victorine poses as a nude sitting with two fully clothed men in this strange, theatrical picture. The scene was set up in Manet's studio, and the group looks as though it is on a stage with a woodland scene backdrop. The woman paddling in the lake is too large in relation to the trees and the nearby boat. When shown at the Salon des Réfuses, the painting caused a scandal. The subject was borrowed from Titian's *Pastoral Concert* (1576) and the poses from an engraving of Raphael's *The Judgement of Paris*; but people were outraged by the fact that the men are in contemporary dress and the women are not goddesses. The triangular group looks unnatural, especially as Victorine ignores her companions and looks at us.

THE STREET SINGER
Edouard Manet; 1862; 175.2 x 108.5 cm (5 ft 9 in x 3 ft 6 in)
Manet matched the shape of his canvases to his subjects. *Portrait of Victorine Meurent* is square, *Woman Playing a Guitar* horizontal, and, as befits a standing figure, this painting is a tall vertical. Victorine poses, guitar in hand, as a street entertainer walking from one café to the next and eating cherries as she goes. We are positioned near her feet so that she appears statuesque. Inspiration for the painting came after Manet saw a girl emerge from a cabaret bar; she refused to pose for the picture, so he turned to Victorine. This is obviously a studio picture; Manet makes no attempt to provide a convincing context, but treats his subject with great sympathy.

Canvas shape

Iɴ ᴛᴏᴡɴѕ ᴀɴᴅ ᴄɪᴛɪᴇѕ we are surrounded by rectangles; they are so commonplace that we scarcely see them. We notice a book, table, or window only when its shape is unusual; otherwise we simply use it. Paintings have often been described as windows onto an imaginary world and, unless it differs from the norm, we pay little attention to the shape of a picture, preferring to concentrate on what it portrays. Most paintings are rectangular because this shape is the most flexible as well as the most invisible. You can lay a rectangle on its side or place it upright, make it almost square and very stable, or elongate two sides to make it as long and narrow as a ruler. Rectangles are described as "landscape" if they are horizontal and "portrait" if they are upright.

SELF-PORTRAIT
Rembrandt van Rijn; 1661–62; 114.3 x 95.2 cm (45 x 37½ in)
Whether standing or sitting, the human figure fits into a vertical format. The Dutch painter Rembrandt (1606–69) is especially famous for the self-portraits that he made throughout his life. Although he produced nearly a hundred, he almost always used one of two shapes; either an oval or a rectangle. He was 55 years old when he painted this wonderful likeness of himself in the studio, holding his brushes and palette. Attention is focused on his face; the rest is painted rather sketchily.

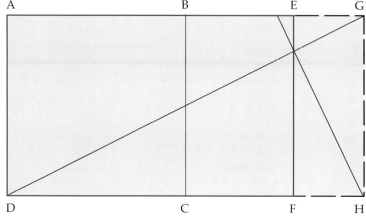

PRINCIPLE OF THE GOLDEN RATIO
Some rectangles are more pleasing to the eye than others. The ancient Greeks based their temples and sculptures on a set of proportions intended to reflect the harmony of the universe. Artists and architects continued to use the ratio in the Middle Ages and the Renaissance, when it was named the Golden Ratio and was considered divine. According to this ratio, if a line is divided in two, the proportion (point of division) works out at roughly 8:13, or just under two-thirds along. While the mathematics are rather complicated, it is possible to construct a rectangle whose sides are in the Golden Ratio without too much difficulty. Draw two adjoining squares ABCD and BGHC. Draw the diagonal DG; draw a line from H to intersect DG at right angles; draw a vertical line EF. This gives you the Golden Rectangle AEFD.

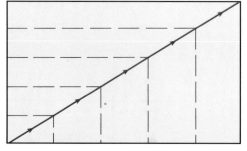

EQUAL PROPORTIONS
It is easy to enlarge or reduce a rectangle while at the same time retaining its proportions. Simply extend the diagonal. If you start with a Golden Rectangle, all further rectangles you create will have Golden Ratio proportions.

An Autumn Landscape with a View of Het Steen

PETER PAUL RUBENS

1636; 131.2 x 229.2 cm (4 ft 4 in x 7 ft 6 in); oil on wood

This painting illustrates how an artist can use a horizontal format to evoke the breadth and depth of a landscape. It shows the estate that the Flemish painter Peter Paul Rubens (1577–1640) bought in 1635. His large house is visible through the trees. Below it are a horse and cart and, in the foreground, a hunter stalking game. All the details are confined to the left-hand side of the picture. To the right of the trees the space opens out to encompass a glorious sweep of countryside. One's eye is led back to the town of Antwerp, tiny on the far horizon.

CHRIST IN THE TOMB

Hans Holbein the Younger; 1521; 30.5 x 200 cm (1 ft x 6 ft 6 in); oil and tempera on wood
The rectangle can be exaggerated to become an expressive element of the composition rather than a neutral frame. The celebrated portrait painter Hans Holbein (1497–1543) portrays the dead Christ in a panel the shape of a tomb. Holbein was a realist. His model was a corpse, and he has not softened the impact of this image of death. Christ lies prone inside the narrow box: feet splayed, chin sticking up, eyes half open. Escape from this confined space seems impossible.

NUDE GIRL

Gwen John; 1909–10; 44.5 x 28 cm (19½ x 11 in)
Female nudes are normally portrayed in poses of relaxed sensuality. To support her painting, Gwen John (1876–1939) worked as an artist's model – she posed for Auguste Rodin – and knew from experience that modelling can be boring, painful, and embarrassing. She shows Fenella Lovell perched awkwardly on a chair – a long, thin shape isolated within a tall, narrow rectangle that echoes her slim proportions. The vertical emphasis makes her seem nervous and vulnerable.

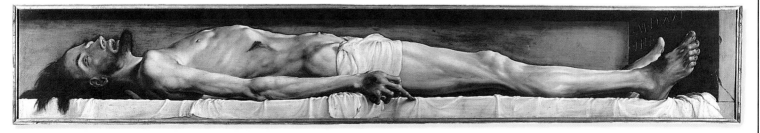

Leading the eye

A PICTURE IS SUCCESSFUL when every detail falls into place and each element – light, tone, colour, texture, form, and spacing – helps to create a clear and lucid image. Every inch of this painting by the Dutch artist Pieter de Hooch (1629–1684) contributes to the design. A woman chooses some bread from a boy's basket. De Hooch leads your eye past them into a courtyard and through an arch to the canal bank, where a neighbour watches from her doorway. Maybe she sent the boy around to the house. Areas of sandy colour – the tiles, the dais under the chair, the cushion and curtains, the house opposite – also lead the eye in a circular movement.

Vanishing point *Horizon line*

Light from the courtyard shines on the woman's face

PAINTING STRUCTURE
A great deal of work goes into making things fit effortlessly into place. A picture must be organized on the surface and into depth, and the two made to work together. Here geometry has been used to define the space. A grid structures the surface (the placing of doors and windows) while perspective recession (pp. 28–29) creates a sense of depth. The two schemes meet in a line running across the bottom of the window and along the courtyard wall to the vanishing point beside the woman in the doorway.

VISUAL LINK
A woman, framed in a doorway on the far bank, looks towards us. Her gaze links foreground and background (the surface and the interior), while her curiosity mirrors ours.

COLOUR PLAY
The woman's red skirt is the only intense colour in the picture; her black jacket is also the darkest area. So as not to compete for attention, the boy is dressed in brownish-grey midtones. The two are united by the light from the courtyard that illuminates her face, his head and shoulders, and the basket of bread.

ATTENTION TO DETAIL
De Hooch loved painting light shining onto walls and through windows. Here a pattern of blue leaves and birds frames two shields; on the left is the name Cornelis Jansz and the trademark of the man's family, on the right that of the woman's family and the name Marnic or Maerti – indicating the occupants of this quiet and ordered home. Through the leaded window one can see the house opposite, glowing golden in the sunlight, with its orange curtains echoing the half curtains of this interior.

A Boy Bringing Bread

PIETER DE HOOCH *1664; 73.5 x 59 cm (29 x 23¾ in)*

De Hooch's delightful painting shows a simple domestic scene. A boy has brought a basket of bread and the woman of the house chooses a loaf. It is the kind of event that happens every day; the very ordinariness of the scene is its charm. But by treating the subject with enormous poise and dignity, de Hooch creates a painting that celebrates the pleasures of a quiet life in which simple activities are valued and enjoyed. Lucid geometry establishes a calm and ordered setting, while gentle sunlight infuses the scene with warm colours that suggest peace and well-being; it is hard to imagine anything disrupting the tranquillity of this household, which seems so remote from the speed and noise of contemporary life.

Placing the figure

A SINGLE FIGURE ISOLATED on a rectangular canvas is one of the simplest compositions; so simple that it might seem as if few options are open to the artist working with this format. But there are crucial decisions to be made on the relationship between the figure and the background. The subject can be silhouetted on a flat surface, situated in a three-dimensional space like a room, or left to establish his or her own volume within an ambiguous field of colour. Manet chose a square canvas for his *Portrait of Victorine Meurent* and placed her head in the centre, so that she dominates the space. In Van Gogh's (1853–90) *Self-Portrait*, the background and figure are of equal importance.

PORTRAIT OF VICTORINE MEURENT
Edouard Manet; 1862; 43 x 43 cm (17 x 17 in)
Manet's portrait of Victorine Meurent is divided into two distinct areas: the model's light head and shoulders, and the dark ground framing her. The background is empty but it is not formless; the square format of the canvas gives it a distinctive shape. Victorine's head and the surrounding space interlock like pieces of a jigsaw puzzle.

DIALOGUE OF OPPOSITES
The drama of the design comes from establishing a dialogue between opposites: dark/light, empty/full, flat/three-dimensional. The warm brown of the flat background offsets the volume of the head. Golden shadows down Victorine's cheek and neck, and underneath her nose and chin, create a sense of solidity. Light makes her forehead, nose, and chin seem to project.

OI YOI YOI
Roger Hilton; 1963; 152.4 x 127 cm (5 ft x 4 ft 1 in)
Roger Hilton originally painted abstract pictures in which each area of the canvas is given equal prominence, since there is no need to distinguish between the "figure" and the "ground". Hilton carries this principle through into this joyful painting of a leaping woman who is treated as an empty shape surrounded by areas painted in vibrant, primary colours so as to appear as important as the figure. Even so, the woman still dominates the composition.

Self-Portrait

VINCENT VAN GOGH *1889; 65 x 54 cm (25½ x 21¼ in)*
Van Gogh painted this extraordinarily intense self-portrait
while he was recovering from a mental breakdown in
the asylum at St. Rémy in Provence. Painting helped him
recover. "I am working like one actually posessed", he
wrote to his brother. "I am in a dumb fury of work. And
I think that this will help cure me." The doctor diagnosed
his fits as a form of epilepsy. "During the attacks", wrote
Van Gogh, "I feel a coward before the pain and suffering ...
I also feel very frightened". His anguish is almost palpable
and seems to have permeated his whole environment.
Every inch of the canvas is awash with emotionally-
charged brushwork so that little distinction is made
between the artist and his surroundings.

BACKGROUND SWIRLS

The wall is painted with the
same swirls that animate
the artist's coat and is
coloured a similar blue-
green. The patterns are
like water and remind
one that emotional
upheaval is often
described as being
"all at sea". Van Gogh
wrote that he was, "like
a man who meant to
commit suicide and,
finding the water too
cold, tries to regain
the bank". The painting
suggests that he is still adrift
in a sea of emotional turmoil.

AN OBVIOUS AFFLICTION

Sickness permeates the
picture. The shadows beneath
the artist's eyes are tinged a livid
green, his lips have green lights,
and his forehead, nose, and
cheek have a yellow palour;
everything seems jaundiced.
The pain in his eyes and
tension in his head and neck
are virtually tangible, as though
he were bracing himself for
another attack. The head is the
only solid form in the picture,
everything else seems to be
dissolving in a wash of anxiety.

DISTINGUISHING BEARD

The red of the artist's beard
and hair helps to differentiate
his head from the wall behind.
The texture of hair is evoked
with shorter, straighter marks
than the swirls washing over
the rest of the canvas.

A CERTAIN EDGINESS

The whole picture seems
afflicted with nervous tension and
the surface is alive with excitable
brushmarks. One's eyes wander
over the canvas, searching in
vain for a resting place, before
returning to the intense eyes
of the artist – which peer like
a hawk, watching for signs of
recurring madness. The pain and
tension are almost unbearable.

Symmetry/asymmetry

Faces, flowers, fruit – symmetry is a natural phenomenon. Or is it? The two sides of a face are surprisingly different. If each side is repeated to make exactly symmetrical versions, the two faces look like different people. Our bodies may look symmetrical, but we don't experience them as such. Most of us use one hand and foot far more than the other, and we are conscious of our hearts being off-centre. Our relationship to symmetry is therefore ambivalent. A symmetrical composition, around a central axis, is very pleasing if, like our faces, it contains minor differences; but perfect symmetry, in which one half of a picture mirrors the other exactly, can seem either boring or uncanny. It is also very static. Asymmetry, in which there's an obvious difference between the two halves, is a more dynamic option, but it requires a subtle balancing act of another kind if the imbalance is to appear interesting rather than awkward.

Point of balance and centre of composition

THE VIRGIN AND CHILD WITH SAINTS GEORGE AND ANTHONY ABBOT
Antonio Pisanello; mid-15th century; 47 x 29 cm (18½ x 11½ in); egg tempera on wood
The Virgin and Child appear in the orb of the sun, whose warmth radiates out in exquisite wave patterns. A line of dark trees at shoulder height separates heaven from earth, the vision from the two saints. St. George wears elegant silver armour decorated with gold trim; wrapped around his legs is a snarling dragon. His broad-brimmed hat echoes St. Anthony Abbot's halo. The older man is accompanied by his attributes – a hog and the bell rung by his order to summon alms from the faithful.

BALANCE OF OPPOSITES
Pisanello's composition pivots around a central vertical axis running through the Virgin, bell, and hog. The saints are balanced as evenly as the figures on a revolving weather vane – St. Anthony faces us and St. George turns away. It is a balance of opposites: dark/light, old/young, bearded/clean-shaven, humbly dressed/flamboyant. Even the plants grow in a symmetrical pattern, but the horses heads break the symmetry. Symmetry gives equal weight to the two sides of a painting as surely as a well-balanced pair of scales. It was used by some artists as a symbol of divine harmony (pp. 16–17).

14

Mr. and Mrs. Andrews

THOMAS GAINSBOROUGH

1748; 70 x 119 cm (27½ x 46¾ in)

The famous English portrait artist Thomas Gainsborough (1727–88) painted these newlyweds on their farm in Suffolk. It was unusual for him to place his sitters in a real landscape, so this picture must be a celebration of ownership. This may explain the picture's asymmetry, with the vast sweep of land on the right and the couple placed to one side on the left. The couple look as though they are in a garden – the young wife would not be willing to venture far in her gown and satin slippers – yet the cornfield is only a few feet away. With his gun under his arm and dog by his side, the master looks far more at home in these surroundings than his wife.

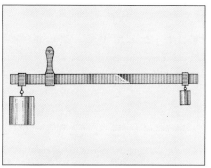

A CENTRAL PIVOT

The tree is the fulcrum of the composition. It anchors the figures, whose mass is balanced on the far right by three spindly trees and a clump of wheat sheaves. The principle is similar to that of a steelyard (p. 62) in which an object is balanced by a small weight, out on a limb.

Compositional centre of balance

The tree acts as a fulcrum

Centre of the canvas

Slender trees and wheat sheaves balance the figures

The blue hooped skirt echoes the curve of the garden seat

Sacred geometry

How can composition be used to make a statement of religious belief? Artists in Renaissance Italy were keen to celebrate the order and harmony that they thought governed the universe, since God's creation must be rational and beautiful. Mathematics was the key; it demonstrated that everything had its place in a logical system, ordered by divine intelligence. In his book of 1435, *On Painting*, the architect and theoretician Leon Battista Alberti applied this belief to painting. He invented the term "composition" to describe the application of mathematics and geometry in organizing all the parts of a picture into a lucid and harmonious design that exemplified the clarity of God's creation. Numbers, therefore, determined the relationship between parts of a painting, certain numbers being considered especially significant: three (Holy Trinity), five (Christ's wounds), and seven (days of the creation).

The Baptism of Christ
PIERO DELLA FRANCESCA
1440–45; 167 x 116 cm (5 ft 6 in x 3 ft 9 in); tempera on wood
Piero della Francesa was a mathematician as well as a painter. The stillness and grandeur of his altarpiece comes from the mathematics governing its design. Christ stands at the centre; the vertical axis runs through the dove and the water trickling from the bowl, to Christ's face, hands, navel, and leg. The composition is based on the ratio of 3:2 – thirds (where the tree and St. John stand) and halves (Christ's loincloth lies where the horizontal division of the square meets the circle).

INTERCONNECTING SHAPES
The clarity and meaning of Piero's picture also comes from its geometry: a circle (heaven, spirit) over a rectangle (earth, matter). Linking the two is the dove (Holy Spirit) placed at the centre of the circle, and along the top of the rectangle. The equilateral triangle enclosing Christ (its apex at his toe) represents the descent of the Holy Spirit; Christ forms the link between heaven and earth, spirit and matter.

Divine symmetry

The sashes float in symmetrical arabesques

The angels poses are almost identical

The angel holds a chalice to collect the blood of Christ

The angels balance on tiny clouds

Christ's body forms the central axis of the composition. The other elements are arranged either side of the cross in almost perfect symmetry (divine perfection). Mary and the saints are placed in standing and kneeling pairs with virtually identical poses. The angels mirror one another in almost every detail, even their glances are paired to create communion between heaven and earth. One angel looks up, the other down. The Virgin and St. John look down at the kneeling saints, who gaze heavenward.

🖌 TONAL SYMBOLISM
The sun and moon above the cross indicate Christ's immortality (his conquest of time) and his dominion over the realms of day and night, life and death, good and evil. To reiterate the idea, the angels wear dark and light, respectively.

🖌 CLEANSING BLOOD
The angels collect the blood flowing from Christ's wounds. Raphael emphasizes Jesus's role as a redeemer, washing away our sins with his blood. He portrays a world cleansed of guilt, sorrow, and sin.

🖌 ULTIMATE SACRIFICE
The garments of Mary and the saints balance light against dark and sorrow against joy, since Christ's supreme sacrifice brings joy to humankind.

🖌 SUPPORTING ROLES
Mary Magdalene and St. Jerome are each associated with atonement. The stone in St. Jerome's hand indicates his years spent in the desert in penance and prayer; his chest is exposed so he can beat his breast. The theme of the painting is redemption through sacrifice.

THE CRUCIFIED CHRIST WITH THE VIRGIN MARY, SAINTS, AND ANGELS
Raphael; 1502; 280.7 x 165.1 cm (9 ft 1¼ in x 5 ft 3½ in)
Raphael's altarpiece, dedicated to St. Jerome, is a devotional image designed for prayer and meditation. The Virgin and St. John stand on either side of the cross while St. Jerome and Mary Magdalene kneel in contemplation of Christ's sacrifice. The calm and balanced composition creates a profound sense of peace, order, and harmony. The clear light and brilliant colour give no hint of Christ's suffering. This serene picture is consoling rather than realistic.

FOREGROUND REALITY
The cross, mourners, and angels are set against an idyllic Umbrian landscape with no middle ground to connect the two realms. This is a devotional image, not quite of this world. The saints act as mediators between us and the realm of divinity, kneeling before the cross just as worshippers knelt before the painting.

Triangular designs

AN EQUILATERAL TRIANGLE, which has sides of equal length, is one of the most stable shapes. Because the apex is centred over the base, the vertical axis divides the triangle into symmetrical halves. The French painter Paul Cézanne (1839–1906) structured his largest painting, *The Great Bathers*, around an equilateral triangle; Renaissance artists, in particular those depicting religious subjects, were similarly attracted to the shape. The triangle is one of the most important Christian symbols; it represents the Holy Trinity – God the Father, the Son, and Holy Ghost. For this reason, two of the most important events in the New Testament, Christ's birth and death (the Madonna and Child and the Crucifixion) are frequently portrayed in compositions governed by triangles, to emphasize the spiritual significance of the event.

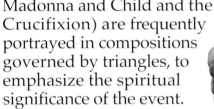

The Madonna's sloping shoulders rise above the horizon and echo the curve of the distant hills

The cross directs one's eye to the apex of the main triangle

The infants regard each other seriously, as though conscious of their destiny

Madonna of the Meadows

RAPHAEL *1505; 113 x 87 cm (44½ x 34¼ in)*

The Madonna and Child is one of the most celebrated subjects in Italian Renaissance art. In a three-year period Raphael (1483–1520) completed 17 works in which the Madonna or the Holy Family were the main subjects. Here the Virgin is placed in an Umbrian landscape; the expanse of water in the background is Lake Trasimeno near Perugia, which would have been familiar to the painter's audience. By placing Mother and Child in a local context, Raphael emphasizes the relevance to his viewers of the Christian story. The Virgin dominates the space with her stable and consoling presence. St. John the Baptist offers his cousin, Jesus, a bamboo cross yet, despite this reminder of the Crucifixion, the mood of the painting is calm and serene.

VIRGIN TRIANGLE
Even though equilateral triangles have a pleasing stability, they are a rather static shape. Raphael's Virgin forms a triangle taller than it is wide, giving her added height and grace. She sits at an angle to us, her pose enlivened by the twist of her head and body. Jesus, whom she gently supports, is framed within this protective triangle. St. John shifts attention from the vertical axis of mother and child to make the composition more dynamic.

Every element of Raphael's picture draws attention to the triangles that structure the composition

The tree frames a triangle of sky

THE GREAT BATHERS
Paul Cézanne; 1898–1905; 208.5 x 249 cm (6 ft 10 in x 8 ft 2 in)
Like the French Impressionists, Paul Cézanne preferred to work outdoors. But while the Impressionists wanted to record immediate sensations, such as patterns of light on water, Cézanne sought to retain a sense of the underlying structure of things, "to make of Impressionism something solid and durable like the art of the museums." This is one of a celebrated series of bathers paintings, with a triangle at the heart of the composition. The triangle unites the two groups of women and imposes a powerful structure that organizes the scene.

THE CRUCIFIED CHRIST WITH THE VIRGIN MARY, SAINTS, AND ANGELS
Raphael; 1503; 280.7 x 165 cm (9 ft 2 in x 5 ft 5 in)
The triangle, symbol of the Holy Trinity, governs the composition of Raphael's Crucifixion. The saints kneeling at the foot of the cross look upward in gratitude. Their poses and gaze suggest a series of triangles whose apex is at the top of the crucifix. The cross, and Christ's body suspended from it, form two inverted triangles. This exchange (upward and downward) indicates the underlying theme of the painting – the giving and receiving of grace. Most of the triangles are flat on the picture plane, but the saints are arranged in a triangle that introduces a sense of depth.

TRIANGULAR COMPOSITION
Cézanne remarked that in nature one should look for the cone, the sphere, and the cylinder – the underlying shapes. In this painting the figures are subordinated to the overall composition. An equilateral triangle, all of whose angles are 60°, frames a space that is empty save for billowing clouds, while the figures are arranged in the foreground in two triangular groups. They are not treated naturalistically, but as anonymous sculptural forms – elements of a grand design. Unlike Raphael, Cézanne does not use the triangle symbolically to embody religious belief, but to suggest the existence of a harmonious relationship between people and nature.

Curvilinear compositions

BECAUSE THEY HAVE a flat base, squares, rectangles, and triangles appear more anchored and static than circles, whose continuous outlines give an impression of movement and freedom from gravity. Curvilinear compositions are governed by circles or rounded, flowing lines that give the eye little opportunity to rest, and create a sensation of endless movement across the surface or back into depth. On a visit to Italy, the Flemish master Peter Paul Rubens (1577–1640) was impressed by the spatious and dynamic compositions of Jacopo Tintoretto. Rubens loved to paint hunting and battle scenes in which he could demonstrate his wizardry at capturing the excitement of a struggle. While his pictures seem chaotic, they are actually brilliantly composed. Tintoretto specialized in showing the movement of bodies through space and painting ceilings in which people fly weightlessly across the heavens.

THE RAPE OF THE DAUGHTERS OF LEUCIPPUS
Peter Paul Rubens; 1618; 224 x 211 cm (7 ft 3 in x 6 ft 9 in)
Rubens's portrayal of the mythic abduction of the daughters of King Leucippus by the twin demigods Castor and Pollux is based on opposites – the blond hair and pale flesh of the women contrasts with the dark hair and swarthy limbs of the captors.

REVEALING AN ORDER
At first sight this painting looks like a frenzied tangle of limbs, but the composition is highly ordered. Four circles, whose centres are at the corners, dissect the space. The lower woman arches around one circle, and the leg and back of the upper woman rest on the two upper circles (right). The struggle seems wild and desperate, but the action is confined within a shallow space framed by the huge bulk of the two horses. The men's gaze binds the four heads in a triangle that provides another anchor to the composition (below). Their look is so determined that it seems to conquer the will of their defenceless victims. The cupid suggests that the attack is motivated by love.

Flying cloaks and manes increase the sense of urgency and excitement

The fiery horses are symbols of masculine potency and military might

Four circles intersecting at the centre create invisible lines that enfold the bodies of the two women

The picture is finely balanced: the lower woman's right hand and foot rest on her captor's boots, while her left hand almost touches the horse's hoof.

SERPENTINE TWISTS
The focal point of the composition is where the two women's bodies meet. All the lines radiate from here, like curved spokes of a wheel, to suggest their desperate bid to escape from this trap. Their heads, bodies, and limbs twist and turn as they struggle to free themselves from their fierce captors.

The Origin of the Milky Way

JACOPO TINTORETTO

c.1577; 148 x 165 cm (4 ft 9 in x 5 ft 3 in)

This painting is based on an ancient Greek myth. Jupiter holds his son, Hercules, to Juno's breast so that he can drink her milk and gain immortality. (Hercules's mother was a mortal.) The milk spurts upwards to form the stars of the Milky Way and downwards to create lilies. The peacocks are Juno's attendants and the eagle is Jupiter's emblem. Tintoretto's use of flying figures and curvilinear movement dramatizes what could have been a tranquil scene to suggest a clash of wills between Juno and Jupiter. The artist's view of space as fluid rather than fixed anticipates, by a few years, the discoveries of the Italian astronomer Galileo (1564–1642), who observed the Milky Way, described the motion of the planets, and related time to space.

ACTION PICTURE
While Rubens's composition is contained within a circle, Tintoretto's painting is so dynamic that the movement seems to extend beyond the frame. Nothing is fixed: the space is defined by bodies flying through it. Cupids glide in from all sides, Jupiter (Zeus) hovers overhead, and his wife, Juno, rests on a bed of clouds. The only anchor is the diagonal along which the goddess's bed is placed, with its sumptuous drapery.

Dramatic diagonals

A POWERFUL ELEMENT FOR dramatizing the action and opening up the picture is the diagonal. A strong diagonal accent leads the eye rapidly across the picture and back into depth, creating an impression of space, suggesting movement, and giving the figures room to act. Artists in the 17th century competed to impress their audiences with compositions dramatic enough to pull viewers into the picture space and involve them in the action. Many of Rubens's compositions incorporate strong diagonals that give his paintings a marvellous dynamism. Had he lived in the 20th century, Tintoretto would surely have been a film director. He was brilliant at orchestrating huge paintings that portray Biblical stories as though they were Hollywood epics, with vast panoramic sweeps and a cast of thousands. In the days before cinema, paintings were the surest way to create dazzling visual spectacles.

The eagle's wings bisect the composition in a diagonal from top left to bottom right

Prometheus was venerated as a Christ-like figure; his wound recalls the gash in Christ's side caused by a sword

PROMETHEUS BOUND
Peter Paul Rubens, 1612–18; 244 x 209.5 cm (8 ft x 6 ft 10½ in)
According to Greek myth, the giant Prometheus stole fire from Mount Olympus and gave it to humankind. In punishment Zeus, the supreme ruler of gods and mortals, chained him to a rock where his liver was devoured by an eagle. Every night it was restored only to be torn out again the next day, so the punishment was eternal. For maximum dramatic effect, Rubens has suspended Prometheus below the diagonal, as though his body were hung from an imaginary line, like an animal strung on a pole – indicating that he is living prey. The flaming torch, bottom left, indicates Prometheus's crime – stealing fire from the gods. The eagle was painted by Frans Snyders, one of Rubens's assistants.

CANOPY OF PAIN
The giant twists toward us in agony. There is little to support his weight, so the body seems suspended from the hook-shaped beak and the sharp talons of the voracious bird that is perched on the diagonal. The bird's wings are spread above the giant like a canopy of perpetual pain. The body is aligned from the bottom right to the top left of the picture, but it also recedes in space with dramatic foreshortening (p. 62), which increases the tension and sense of anguish.

THE LAST SUPPER

Jacopo Tintoretto; 1591; 365 x 568 cm (12 ft x 18 ft 9 in)

Leonardo da Vinci portrays the Last Supper (pp. 28–29) as a calm scene of order and harmony; here Tintoretto dramatizes the event. He sets the table at an acute angle back along the diagonal, places Christ halfway down the room, then uses other elements of the composition to point him out. His head is haloed in light and a host of angels swirls towards him in the lamplight. Two levels of reality exist side-by-side: the ordinary business of serving and eating a meal – the woman kneeling in the foreground dishes out plates of food, while the cat tries to steal a tasty morsel – and the symbolic ritual of breaking bread and drinking wine, which represent the Eucharist, the body and blood of Christ.

JOURNEY AROUND THE PICTURE

Our eyes are drawn backward along the table and are returned to the foreground by the arc of people serving dinner on the right. The circle is completed by the woman kneeling in the centre and the cat stealing food. The woman and the angels above her head all incline towards Christ, who stands behind the table surrounded by radiant light. He is the link between daily life, shown in the lower half of the picture, and the realm of the spiritual portrayed in the upper half.

Shaped paintings

Sometimes artists have to work within an existing format; at other times they opt for an unusual shape. Each shape has its own dynamics, and these affect the design. The French painter Henri Matisse (1869–1954) wrote that composition "alters itself according to the surface to be covered; if I take a sheet of paper of given dimensions, I will jot down a drawing which will have a necessary relation to its format". We have seen that a rectangle is the most flexible shape (pp. 8–9), able to dramatically alter its own proportions and accommodate almost any composition. A square is very stable because all its sides are equal, but this imposes a rather static set of options that are difficult to deal with. Ovals were popular for portraits, especially miniatures designed to be worn from a chain or kept in a pocket. Renaissance paintings of the Madonna and Child are often circular, a shape that symbolizes unity and embodies the indissoluble link between mother and infant.

Christ is flanked by the Virgin Mary

Christ's halo is in relief, like an arch

CRUCIFIX
Style of Segna di Bonaventura; c.1298; 213.5 x 184 cm (7 ft x 6 ft) total size
In the Middle Ages large crucifixes were often hung over the altar of the church. The shape of the cross, outlined in gold that glowed in the candlelight, was as important as the painted image of Christ. In this crucifix, Jesus is watched over by the Virgin and St. John, who mourn his terrible suffering. Initially there was probably a roundel above the cross showing God the Father looking down on his son.

This is the most voluptuous of Raphael's Madonnas

This is the chubbiest of Raphael's infants

The rectangular frame stabilizes the circular painting

MADONNA OF THE CHAIR
Raphael; 1514; 71 cm (28 in) diameter; oil on wood
The Renaissance painter Raphael fits his Madonna and Child beautifully into the circular, or tondo, format. The only upright in the composition is the back of the chair on which the Virgin sits sideways to us. She and the baby intertwine in a series of interlocking S-shaped curves. The circles of her halo and head scarf, the oval of her face, the slope of her neck, the curves of her shoulder, arm, and thigh, and the chubbiness of the baby all echo the motif of the circle. Raphael does not only employ curving lines over the surface, but fills out the bodies of Mother and Child to create solid volumes that reiterate the theme of roundness and plenitude to provide a voluptuous sense of security.

The truncated
corners hem the
animals in

The corners also
lead your eye
from the edges
back to the
centre

Horse Attacked by a Lion

GEORGE STUBBS *1769; 24.3 x 28.2 cm (9⅝ x 11⅛ in); enamel on copper*
The English painter George Stubbs (1724–1806) was
renowned for his anatomical studies and paintings of
racehorses. The theme of a horse being attacked by a lion
preoccupied him for over 30 years. One inspiration was
an antique sculpture of a lion mauling a horse, which he
saw on a visit to Rome; another witness describes him
seeing a Barbary horse being attacked by a lion on the
coast of Africa when he stopped off on his return journey.
Stubbs made 17 works on the subject, including this little
painting in enamel on copper. Despite its small scale
and jewel-like brilliance of colour, the picture has the
flamboyant romanticism of a grand painting. The
wild terror of the pale horse trying to escape the dark
marauder is made palpable by the octagonal shape,
which chops off the corners, hems in the animal, and
directs the viewer's eye back to the centre and the fierce
attack. The horse seems pinned to the spot by its tail and
the S-shaped curve of its body, as much as by the lion.

TARGOWICA III
*Frank Stella; 1973; 310 x 244 x
20.5 cm (10 ft 2 in x 8 ft x 8 in);
mixed media on board*
Instead of treating a
painting as a window
onto an imaginary world,
the American artist Frank
Stella (born 1936) draws
attention to it as a flat
surface. His pictures come in
all shapes – from rectangles
and squares to trapeziums,
zigzags, and star forms.
Bands of colour follow the
edge of each canvas to
emphasize the geometry of
the composition. Here felt
and cardboard add texture
to the surface of the arrow-
shaped object and suggest
the dynamic interlocking
of forms, which look as
though they could adopt
a different configuration.

The horizon

THE HORIZON, the meeting of land or sea with the sky, is so fundamental to our experience that an abstract painting can be transformed into a landscape simply by dividing it with a horizontal line. Because the earth is spherical, the horizon is curved; but the arc is so gentle that we are unaware of it. Most artists portray it as a straight line parallel to the upper edge of the picture. A curve would disrupt the composition and destroy the reassurance offered by the horizon, which functions like a spirit level: confirmation that we are upright. Simulate the tilt of the horizon on a video screen, and viewers will soon feel queasy. In cities we scarcely see the horizon, but in the country we take our bearings from it. Pilots rely on it to tell them if they are flying level. Artists usually place the horizon near the mid-point of their paintings. Raising, lowering, or tilting the line substantially affects the mood of the scene to create a sense of tension or unease. The horizon is at the same height as the viewer's eye level. If it is placed low, everything in the picture towers above us; if it is placed high, we survey the scene from above.

A HERDSMAN WITH COWS BY A RIVER
Aelbert Cuyp; 1650; 45.4 x 74 cm (17⅞ x 29⅛ in)
The Dutch painter Aelbert Cuyp (1620–91) specialized in rural scenes bathed in a golden glow that creates a sense of calm well-being, often enhanced by the presence of a herd of cows. Here the low horizon allows him a vast expanse of luminous sky whose subtle light is reflected off the water.

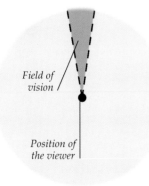

Field of vision

Position of the viewer

LIMITED VIEWPOINT
If you keep your eyes still, only a small section of the horizon at the centre of your field of vision is in focus. We overcome this limitation by scanning our surroundings.

SKETCH FOR HADLEIGH CASTLE
John Constable; 1828–29; 122.5 x 167.5 cm (4 ft x 5 ft 6 in)
Constable (1776–1837) painted this stormy picture soon after the death of his wife, whom he loved dearly. The view past the ruined castle is along the bank of the Thames to the Kent coast and the distant sea. The horizon is set just below the mid-point of the picture and, because there is no land in the foreground, the viewer seems suspended like a bird in an expanse of windswept space extending to the distant meeting of sky and sea. The ruined tower stands alone, battered by the elements. The painting seems symbolic: the ruin clings to the edge of life, while the empty horizon suggests death and eternity.

BRANCH LINE
The branches fill the sky, following the contours of the hills. Employing the same oranges and greens as in the foreground, Cézanne uses the branches both to frame the distance and to emphasize the picture surface.

NEUTRAL PEAK
Because of its colour, the peak seems to belong as much to the sky above the horizon as to the earth beneath it.

FADING COLOUR
Patches of green and orange alternate across the valley floor, becoming paler and less intense the further away they seem. Lines defining fields, hedges and roads also direct one's eye towards the mountain and into depth. To establish its distance and to differentiate it from the flat land below the horizon, the peak is painted in soft blues, purples, and pinks.

HIDDEN HORIZON
The peak rises above the horizon, but Cézanne retains a sense of where the horizon line would be (below). The diagonals intersect on the horizon, and the colour alters at this level from the oranges and greens used to describe the valley, to the blues and pinks defining the mountain.

Mont Sainte-Victoire

PAUL CÉZANNE *1887; 66.8 x 92.3 cm (26 x 36¼ in)*

Cézanne was obsessed with this mountain near his home in Aix-en-Provence. He painted it again and again over a period of 30 years. He enjoyed painting outdoors in front of the subject, but this does not mean that the picture was spontaneous. Infra-red photographs reveal an under drawing in Prussian blue paint, used to work out the composition. Cézanne was keen to achieve two contradictory things: to create a convincing illusion of depth and also to retain awareness of the painting as a flat surface. A combination of line and colour creates the impression of distance across the valley, while the tree on the left and its branches frame the view and draw one's attention back to the foreground. The triangular mountain hides the horizon, but Cézanne indicates its location with a change of colour and line. Green and orange change to blue and pink, and straight lines to curves.

The vanishing point

CENTRAL FIGURE
Christ forms a triangle, whose three sides symbolize the Holy Trinity (pp. 18–19). He is centred at the vanishing point, so all lines lead towards him. Perspective is used here as a demonstration of Christian principles.

In 1435 THE FLORENTINE architect and theoretician Leon Battista Alberti published *On Painting*, outlining the basic rules of perspective. These rules were used to make a convincing picture of things as seen by a single viewer from a fixed position. Parallel lines, like the sides of a road, appear to converge as they recede into the distance. Theoretically they meet in infinity, at a point called the vanishing point. The same rule also applies to horizontal lines: the roof and the base of a house converge towards infinity so that the building seems to diminish in height towards the far end, just like the trees lining the avenue in Meindert Hobbema's (1638–1709) famous landscape. Orthogonals are the lines that map these convergences. The horizon is at the viewer's eye level, and the vanishing point is on the horizon directly in front of the viewer. If the artist places it dead centre, it is like a bull's eye, insistently drawing the eye towards it.

The Last Supper

LEONARDO DA VINCI *1495–97; 460 x 880 cm (15 ft x 28 ft 10 in); tempera and oil on ground limestone*
Leonardo da Vinci painted his *Last Supper* on the wall of the dining room of the Convent of Santa Maria Della Grazie, Milan, to give the impression that the meal is taking place in an upper room. He uses perspective to create space and depth, but also to illustrate religious belief. Christ is placed at the centre; the vanishing point is located on his forehead – he embodies infinity. The disciples are clustered along the horizon in four groups of three: symbolic numbers that also emphasize the spiritual significance of the event.

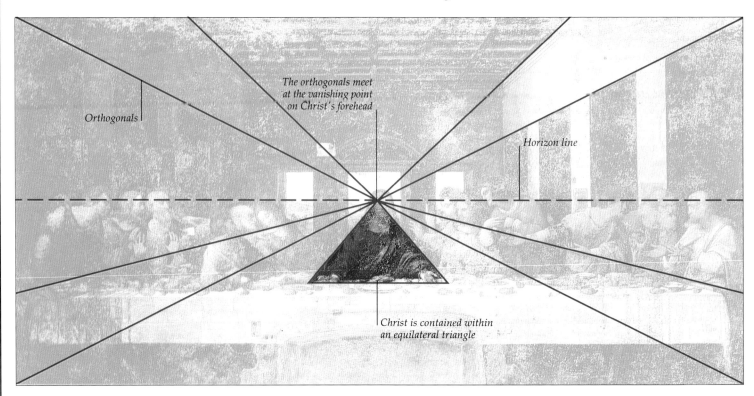

Orthogonals

The orthogonals meet at the vanishing point on Christ's forehead

Horizon line

Christ is contained within an equilateral triangle

The Avenue, Middelharnis

MEINDERT HOBBEMA
1689; 103.5 x 141 cm (40¾ x 55½ in)

Hobbema specialized in landscapes featuring woodland glades and thatched cottages surrounded by massive trees. This more open view, with its dramatic foreshortening (p. 62), is something of a departure. The horizon is clearly visible across the meadows. The head of the man walking towards us is on the horizon line, so his eye level matches ours – as though he is inviting us to join him.

A LOW HORIZON
The low horizon allows Hobbema to silhouette the tall trees flanking the road against an enormous expanse of sky. The orthogonals draw your eye along the road towards the vanishing point, located just off centre. Hobbema is not, like Leonardo, making a religious point; he is simply adding drama to a sleepy rural scene.

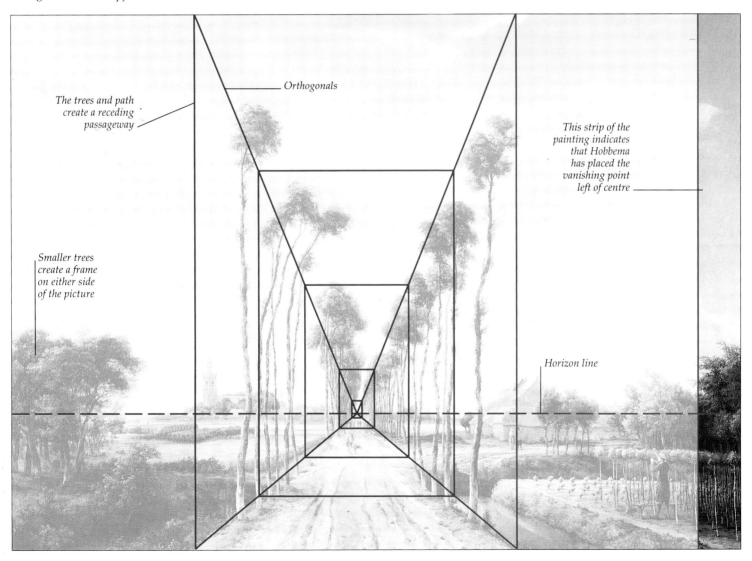

Orthogonals

The trees and path create a receding passageway

This strip of the painting indicates that Hobbema has placed the vanishing point left of centre

Smaller trees create a frame on either side of the picture

Horizon line

Moving the horizon

SHIFTING THE vanishing point (pp. 28–29) and the horizon up or down can create a sense of dynamic tension. In *St. James Led to Execution* Andrea Mantegna (1431–1506) placed the vanishing point below the picture to introduce contradictory accents. The orthogonals (p. 28) draw the eye inexorably down towards the vanishing point, while the exaggerated verticals counter this movement with an upward thrust that generates tension. Raising the vanishing point above the picture's edge also creates a dual movement. Whereas Mantegna's street seems to tip away from us, the surface of the water in Claude Monet's (1840–1926) *Waterlilies* seems to slide into our laps as our eyes glide over the pool, drawn upwards towards the vanishing point.

ST. JAMES LED TO EXECUTION
Andrea Mantegna; 1455; fresco, Eremitani Church, Padua
This scene from a cycle of frescoes by Andrea Mantegna shows St. James being led to his execution by a group of Roman soldiers. The saint has stopped to bless a kneeling penitent, much to the surprise of the soldier with his back to us, who is poised at the front of the picture as though he were standing on a ledge. The low viewpoint gives the figures the statuesque volume of sculptures. People watch from windows and, below them, an excited crowd is held back by a soldier. Emotional tension is created by the plummeting lines of the unusual perspective and the upward thrust of the architecture. The triumphal arch that soars overhead is an expression of the might of the Roman Empire. The spiral curve of the banner and the wisps of cloud in the sky indicate the turbulent mood below.

Horizon | Vanishing point

CHANGING THE HORIZON
In this preparatory sketch the perspective is closer to a more conventional composition where the horizon is still within the picture frame; the idea for a dramatically lowered horizon came only in the final stages of planning.

DRAMATIC VIEWPOINT
Mantegna was keen to use his knowledge of perspective for dramatic impact. He places the vanishing point below the picture so that everything is seen from below, oddly foreshortened (p. 62). The vanishing point is indicated by the gazes of the soldier and St. John on the left, and the inverted V between the two soldiers, one in the centre, the other pushing back the crowd on the right.

Waterlilies

CLAUDE MONET *1914;*
130 x 150 cm (50¼ x 58½ in)

The garden created by Claude Monet at Giverny, north-west of Paris, is almost as famous as his paintings. The lake that inspired nearly 80 paintings was 20 metres (65 feet) wide and 60 metres (197 feet) long. It was fringed with bamboo, rhododendron, apple and cherry trees, and waterlilies floated on its surface. Reflections in water and light playing over its surface are recurring themes in Monet's work. "The essence of the motif," he said, "is the mirror of water whose appearance changes at every moment because areas of sky are reflected in it." There are no banks to anchor the picture, so we are sucked into a vibrant mirage of illusory surfaces and depths.

BEGUILING SCENE
The shimmering reflections in the water – a favourite subject of Monet's – turn everything upside down. When viewed this way up, it seems to be a painting of reeds and sky. Only the lily pads indicate that this is a reflection. This intoxicating spectacle is further complicated by the fact that the painting has no horizon line. The high vanishing point draws one's eye towards the top of the picture as though you were a dragonfly skimming the surface, while the water seems to flow towards us.

Golden Section

GOLDEN RATIO IN NATURE
A nautilus shell grows according to Golden Section proportions, as do sunflower seeds, dandelions, dahlias, and pine cones.

THE ANCIENT GREEKS believed that proportion in both art and life led to health and beauty. In his book *The Elements* (300 BC) Euclid demonstrated the ratio that Plato called "The Section", which later came to be known as the Golden Section. It formed the basis of Greek art and architecture; the design of the Parthenon in Athens is governed by it. In the Middle Ages the Golden Section was considered divine: it was thought to embody the perfection of God's creation. Renaissance artists frequently employed it as the embodiment of divine logic. Jan Vermeer (1632–75) continued to use it in Holland; but after that interest dwindled until the 1920s, when Piet Mondrian (1872–1944) began to base his abstract paintings on the ratio.

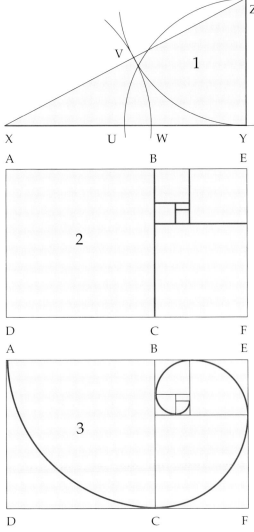

CREATING THE GOLDEN SECTION
(*Fig. 1*) If a line is divided at the Golden Ratio, the smaller part is to the larger as the larger is to the whole. To divide the line XY at the point of the Golden Ratio, divide XY at the centre (U); draw an arc from Y through U to cut through Z (at right angles to XY). Join YZ and XZ. From Z draw an arc through Y to cut XZ at V. From X draw an arc, radius XV, to cut XY at W. XY:XW = XW:WY.
(*Fig. 2*) A rectangle whose sides are in the Golden Ratio (p. 8) can be divided into a square ABCD plus a Golden Rectangle BCFE. This rectangle can also be divided into a square and a Golden Rectangle, and so on ad infinitum.
(*Fig. 3*) By joining the shapes, the repeated divisions give rise to a spiral that duplicates those seen in nature (top left).

THE ARTIST IN HIS STUDIO
Jan Vermeer; 1665; 120 x 100 cm (47¼ x 39⅜ in)
This gorgeous painting seeks to establish Vermeer as a history painter. A tapestry has been drawn back to reveal the artist at work, dressed in late medieval costume. His model represents Clio, the muse of history. She holds the trumpet, wears the laurel wreath of fame, and holds a volume of Thucydides, symbolizing history. The plaster cast on the table represents imitation. The map on the wall shows the Netherlands before they were divided in 1648 into the Protestant north and the Catholic south – the painting probably celebrates the glory of Dutch art before the division. The whole scene is bathed in exquisitely subtle light that pours in through the unseen window to create a superb sense of space and volume.

Golden Section lines

The calm beauty of Vermeer's painting comes from the underlying sense of order. If you chart the placement of key items, you discover that their position is governed by a network of lines based on the Golden Section. The map, chandelier and easel lie on Golden Section divisions; the rectangle framing the artist and model is defined by Golden Section lines that follow the edge of the map, define the position of the curtain, and support the artist's elbow as he paints the picture within a picture. The fact that his arm actually rests on a Golden Section line suggests that Vermeer saw the ratio as one of the mainstays of painting.

DISSECTING THE RECTANGLE
Every line can be divided according to the Golden Ratio in two places. This diagram shows the dynamics of a Golden Section rectangle. Each side has been divided twice to create nine smaller rectangles. If you draw each diagonal, you get a complex web of interrelations resembling a game of cat's cradle. Analysis of Vermeer's painting shows that key elements in the picture are placed on these lines or at the intersections.

Leonardo's Vitruvian man

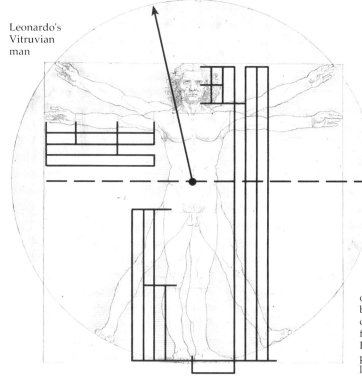

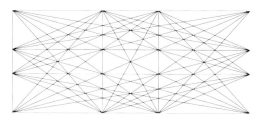

Golden section proportions of the arm and hand

13 — 8 — 5 — 3

16

48 — 32

3 — 2

1

A NATURAL PHENOMENON
Leonardo da Vinci's drawing "The Proportions of the Human Figure" (1492, left) is based on a system of proportion devised by the Roman architect Vitruvius in c.27 AD. Taking the human body as the measure, he proposed a set of relations for use in designing buildings, sculpture, and paintings. "If a man be placed flat on his back", he wrote, "with hands and feet extended, and a pair of compasses centred at his navel, the fingers and toes of his two hands and feet will touch the circumference of a circle." Leonardo's man shows the Golden Proportions found in the human body. On a smaller scale, the ratio occurs between parts of the skeleton (above). If the distance from fingertip to elbow joint is the length of the line, the wrist lies on Golden Section proportions (where 1 = 16 units).

Eye-to-eye contact

NARRATIVE PAINTINGS generally work rather like theatre. While accommodating the audience – not turning their backs on us and making sure that events are visible – the characters, by and large, pretend that we are not there. This allows us to forget ourselves and to become absorbed in the action. Some paintings, though, dramatize the act of looking; the direction of someone's gaze becomes the pivot around which the whole composition is organized. Diego Velázquez (1599–1660), the painter to the Spanish court, enjoyed playing with the idea of who is watching whom and making the viewer aware of their role as spectator. By acknowledging your presence in this way, a fascinating dialogue is established between the imaginary world of the picture and the real space that you occupy.

SELF-PORTRAIT
Rembrandt van Rijn;
1662; 114.5 x 95 cm (45 x 37½ in)
Self-portraits are often unnerving; the artist stares intently out of the picture, as though returning your gaze, when he or she is, of course, peering into a mirror. Such unwavering eye contact would be disconcerting in real life. Rembrandt made nearly a hundred images of himself, creating a memorable record of his life. His eyes seem to look deeply into yours, and are full of wisdom and understanding, as though he wants to share his experiences with you. It is over 300 years since he stood in front of the mirror, but the intensity of this portrait makes him seem present in the room.

ECHOING CURVES
This painting is composed in gentle curves. The curve of Venus's back is echoed by the grey drapery on which she lies; the arc of her leg and hip mirror the upper edge of the bed. The two sets of curves – foreground horizontals and background verticals – meet beneath the kneeling Cupid.

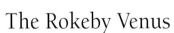

The Rokeby Venus

DIEGO VELAZQUEZ *1651; 120 x 180 cm (4 ft x 5 ft 9 in)*
Reclining nudes traditionally adopt a pose of dreamy languor, or else look invitingly towards the viewer. Venus, on the other hand, is usually shown seated, gazing into a mirror, so that she and the viewer are engaged in the same activity: admiring her beauty. By merging the two conventions, Velázquez sets up an interesting game. Venus lies with her back to us as though she were preoccupied, looking in the mirror. But the image in the glass does not match the slender body and neck in front of us. The face is too round and too ruddy, as though Velázquez were contrasting the actual (a model posing for him) with the ideal (a delicate goddess). The mirror is not held at the right angle for Venus to see her reflection, but is tilted so the young woman can spy on us as we look at her. Velázquez playfully contrasts the myth of a goddess admiring herself with the reality of a model posing for the painting which the viewer enjoys.

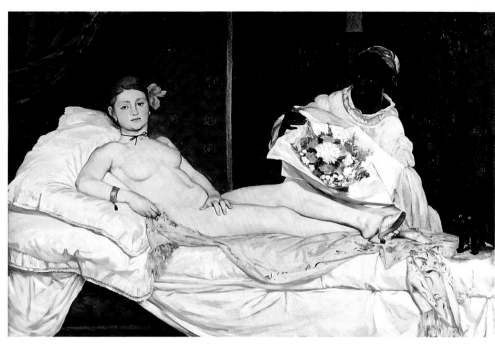

WHO'S LOOKING AT WHOM?
Velázquez sets up an elaborate game in which the viewer interacts with Venus. If you stand in the right place, you get the impression that you are exchanging glances with Venus via the mirror. Instead of being an inanimate object, she becomes a playful participant.

OLYMPIA
Edouard Manet, 1863; 130 x 190 cm (4 ft 3 in x 6 ft)
When it was first shown in Paris in 1865, Manet's painting had to be protected from an angry crowd, outraged by its directness. Manet painted an ordinary woman in high-heeled slippers rather than an imaginary ideal. She stares at us, as though challenging our right to look at her. Manet makes it clear that his model is a person with ideas of her own, making us feel awkward about invading her privacy. She seems to judge us, when normally we would be in a position to appraise her. By reversing power relations between viewer and viewed, Manet makes us feel uncomfortable.

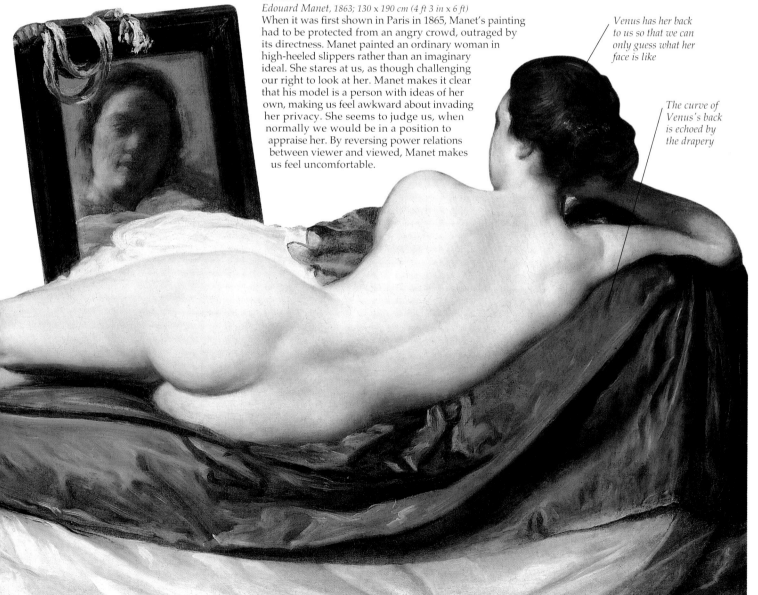

Venus has her back to us so that we can only guess what her face is like

The curve of Venus's back is echoed by the drapery

Sequence of events

PAINTINGS ARE SILENT, flat, and static. How can one hope to capture in them experience of a world that is three-dimensional, moving, and noisy? How does one convey the unravelling of events through time? Peter Bruegel the Elder (1525–69) depicted a single moment of a story (pp. 38–39) yet was able to indicate, through the dynamics of composition, the likely outcome of events. In the Middle Ages artists portrayed time in a more fluid way. Instead of isolating a single incident, they rendered numerous episodes like a comic strip, in overlapping or interconnecting scenes. The Italian Renaissance painter Sandro Botticelli (1445–1510) revived this idea in his Sistine Chapel fresco, which shows various incidents in the life of Moses. Moses appears seven times in a painting that describes events that occurred over several years as though no time had elapsed. It was not until the impact of film in the twentieth century that artists began, once more, to experiment with the idea of showing interrelated events in one picture. The Italian Futurist (p. 62) Umberto Boccioni (1882–1916) tried to describe events happening simultaneously in different places – for instance, street noise heard through an open window.

The Youth of Moses

SANDRO BOTTICELLI *1481–82; fresco, Sistine Chapel*
In 1481 Sandro Botticelli was commissioned by Pope Sixtus IV to decorate the walls of the recently built Sistine Chapel in the Vatican with scenes from the lives of Moses and Christ. Rather than depict the story of Moses as a series of independent scenes, he amalgamated the incidents into one composition, weaving them together spatially as though they were happening simultaneously.

NOISE OF THE STREET ENTERING THE HOUSE
Umberto Boccioni; 1911; 70 x 75 cm (27½ x 29½ in)
In this complicated painting Umberto Boccioni was trying to show that the noise and bustle of the street envelops the woman on the balcony. Everything interconnects. Horses are entwined in the balcony railings, and the workmen in the square and their scaffolding poles are repeated in a pattern that fills the air, like sound, to suggest the clatter of action. The buildings repeat like an echo, as though reflecting the sound waves. On film one would be able to cut from one frame of reference to another; Boccioni relies on juxtaposition and overlap to indicate noisy interaction.

*Making
his escape*

MOSES FLEES
When news of the murder leaked out, Pharaoh ordered Moses to be killed; here Moses is making his getaway to the land of Midian.

*Driving
away the
shepherds*

MOSES PROTECTS
The central pivot of the composition is the well, beside which Moses drives away some shepherds.

*The
murder*

*Returning to
Egypt*

*Kneeling
before God*

MOSES'S MISSION
Moses kneels before God, who appears in a burning bush and tells him to return to Egypt to save the Israelites.

WORD OF GOD
While Moses is guarding Jethro's flock, God appears and tells him to remove his sandals because he is on holy ground.

*Removing
his sandals*

Watering the sheep

JOURNEY TO EGYPT
Moses, guided by the rod of God, takes his family back to Egypt to persuade Pharaoh to release the Israelites. Although several years have passed between the first and last scenes, the seven incidents are linked into a single fluent composition as if no time had elapsed.

A GOOD SAMARITAN
Moses draws water for two of the daughters. On their return home they recounted the story to their father, who invited Moses to stay in his house and to marry his daughter Zipporah. She later bore him a son.

START OF THE NARRATIVE
Moses appears seven times, distinctively dressed in a golden tunic and a dark green mantle, which, top left, he has removed in the sight of the Lord. The story begins here, bottom right, in a vivid cameo that shows Moses killing an Egyptian who has beaten the Israelite being helped away behind him.

Depicting an episode

HOW CAN YOU EXPLAIN the unfolding of a story if you have only one picture in which to do so? Most artists choose a single dramatic moment and hope their audience will be able to imagine the events immediately before and after. The actions, gestures, expressions and placing of the characters, their relationship to one another and their surroundings are crucial signs as to what is happening. In his *Parable of the Blind* the Flemish painter Pieter Bruegel the Elder vividly captures a single moment, but he also indicates the future outcome. The picture illustrates a parable told by Jesus in the Gospel of St. Matthew: "If the blind lead the blind, both shall fall into the ditch." Bruegel shows six blind men stumbling along. The leader has already fallen into the ditch and the composition leaves no doubt that the others will soon tumble after him and land in a pathetic heap. The men, clinging to poles or holding onto one another's shoulders, are strung out in a line with a strong descending diagonal from top left to bottom right of the picture. This creates a momentum that seems to precipitate the fall – as though the figures were propelled down an invisible shaft. The low viewpoint dramatizes their fall.

A LOW VIEWPOINT AND CLOSE UP
Bruegel's powers of observation are extraordinary. He gives us exact portraits of different forms of blindness and conveys what it must be like to be forced to rely on other senses such as sound, touch, and smell. Even so, there is an element of caricature in the drawing that makes the men's predicament seem comic as well as tragic.

PARABLE OF THE BLIND
Peter Bruegel the Elder; 1568;
86 x 154 cm (33¼ x 60½ in); tempera on canvas
The parable of the blind warns people against following false guides. Christ was referring to the Pharisees, a religious group whom he accused of hypocrisy. Bruegel's painting carries a similar message. In the 16th century various religious groups including Anabaptists, Lutherans, and Calvinists sprang up to challenge the Catholic Church, and the painting is probably a warning against these groups. The church prominent in the background is Pede St. Anne, near Brussels. The men stagger past it, oblivious of the guidance it could offer them. The men therefore exemplify folly and inner blindness.

DISTINCT PORTRAITS
Carefully observed details bring the painting to life. This man is suffering from atrophy of the eye muscles, and he turns towards us as though in a desperate plea for help.

This man listens intently, guessing that something is wrong

Bruegel studied various forms of blindness; he portrays in vivid detail glaucoma, cataracts, and atrophy of the eye muscles. His characters are comical, but they also arouse sympathy because their suffering is real

The men are linked by their arms and this pole, which forms one of the strong diagonal lines of the composition that leads them into the ditch

The flowing cloak adds to the sense of movement

This man is on tiptoe as though he is about to fall over

This man has already lost his balance and will soon be in the ditch

A LINE OF BLIND MEN

Bruegel has portrayed the parable literally, as a line of blind men following one another. The figures are very accurately observed. The leader has tumbled into a shallow river and the second man trips over him; the third is about to lose his balance and the fourth hesitates in alarm, sensing danger. The fifth man is oblivious of what lies ahead, while the sixth tags along in blissful ignorance, his lumpy shape and trusting expression suggesting stupidity. The gap between the first two men and the others is like a dramatic pause, a moment of tension before they too topple over. The diagonal composition indicates the immediate outcome; the six will end up as a dishevelled heap in the ditch, with no one to help them.

THE DIAGONAL COMPOSITION

This is brilliant storytelling. While portraying a single moment, Bruegel implies a whole sequence of events. The group files along a ridge surrounded by ditches. They also teeter along between two imaginary lines that form a shaft along the diagonal of the picture from top left to bottom right. The top line runs along the men's arms and the pole that links them. The bottom one follows their feet, so that their fall headlong into the water seems inevitable. The poles link the men to one another and indicate their reliance on touch to find their way about. They are also vital elements in the composition.

Painting as theatre

A THEATRICAL COMPOSITION is like a still from a play. Setting, lighting, and props establish a context within which the characters interact. Because painters do not have sound or movement at their disposal, they have to rely on the dramatic placing of the figures and elements such as posture, gesture, and expression to tell the story and convey emotion. The Italian painter Paolo Veronese (1528–88) set the scene for *The Family of Darius Before Alexander* on the terrace of a Palladian villa watched by people clustered on a balcony, as though the event were staged in an open-air theatre. The Persian king Darius and his family kneel for their lives before Alexander the Great, after the defeat of Darius's army at the Battle of Issus in 33 BC. Veronese emphasizes the idea of a play by casting members of the Pisani family, who commissioned this painting, in the parts of Darius and his family. They are decked in jewels to indicate their wealth and dressed in contemporary Venetian clothes rather than in Persian costume. Inspired by Veronese's example, nearly two hundred years later Giambattista Tiepolo (1696–1770) turned a whole room in a Venetian palace into a dazzling theatrical spectacle based on the story of Anthony and Cleopatra. In *The Banquet of Cleopatra* it is almost impossible to tell where the real architecture ends and the fresco begins.

THE BANQUET OF CLEOPATRA
Giambattista Tiepolo; 1734–50; fresco, Palazzo Labia, Venice
This scene is painted between two real doors. A dwarf leads us up imaginary steps to the banquet. Mark Anthony faces us decked in armour, while Cleopatra is dressed as a Venetian noblewoman. Having promised the most costly dish ever produced, Cleopatra dissolves her pearl earring in a glass of vinegar and drinks it. She is separated from Mark Anthony by the V of the perspective lines which open up an airy central space. The vanishing point is low, so the architecture framing the scene soars above the imaginary stage on which the drama takes place.

A DRAMATIC GESTURE
Hephaestion was Alexander's general and compatriot. Here, he gestures toward the man on his left and the kneeling queen. She has supposedly mistaken Hephaestion for Alexander, and the general indicates that Alexander is, in fact, the man to his left, dressed in shining armour. The queen echoes Hephaestion's gesture. Both indicate someone behind them, so creating a diagonal movement that opens up the shallow space of the terrace.

The guard looks across towards the centre. His gaze and the monkey's bridge the gap in the balustrade

Members of the Pisani family, dressed in their own sumptuous clothes, pose as Darius's family

The chained monkey symbolizes the family's future servitude to Alexander

This guard appears to be standing at the foot of some stairs, preventing access or escape

THE FAMILY OF DARIUS BEFORE ALEXANDER
Paolo Veronese; 1573; 236 x 475 cm (7 ft 9 in x 15 ft 6 in)
The foreground figures are arranged in two groups on a narrow terrace. Darius is at the centre of the composition, his head at the apex of the triangle formed by his kneeling family. He commends them to Alexander with a pleading look and gesture. The queen, her mouth open in speech, offers the conqueror her eldest daughter. With their spears, Alexander's entourage forms a tall triangle indicative of their supremacy.

STAGE POSITIONS

The arrangement of the foreground figures down the diagonal, from the horse's head, top right, to the sentry, bottom left, establishes a line of power from the conquering army down to the defeated civilians. The gesture of Darius's youngest daughter echoes that of her father. She directs the servants behind her to keep still while the negotiations are under way. The brocade train of her sister's dress leads one's eye from the family group back toward the man guarding them in the courtyard below.

The spears form the apex of a triangle, which dramatizes Alexander and Hephaestion

The horse towers over the scene, as a symbol of military might

This inverted triangle of empty space divides the two groups

The queen kneels before Alexander and offers him her daughter

Tonal values

THERE IS NOTHING more dramatic than standing someone in a pool of darkness, then turning a spotlight on them. Lighting directors know the power of light / dark contrast to focus audience attention. The same principle applies in painting – whole compositions can be structured around contrasts of light and dark. In his huge painting *The Night Watch*, the Dutch painter Rembrandt (1606–69) uses the interplay of warm lights and velvety dark to create the impression of a space filled with people. Maximum contrast is established in the costumes of the two main characters. Captain Frans Banning Cocq is dressed in black offset by a red sash and white lace collar; his lieutenant, Willem van Ruytenburgh, wears pale gold. One outfit soaks up the light, the other seems to glow. They are surrounded by figures in more sombre dress; except for the girl in yellow, they are all painted in subtle mid tones.

LIGHT AND SHADE
The captain's hand casts a shadow over his lieutenant's tunic. This detail is important; it establishes the captain in front of his subordinate.

The company's banner, held aloft by an ensign, creates a striking diagonal

The Night Watch

REMBRANDT VAN RIJN *1642; 359 x 348 cm (11 ft 9 in x 11 ft 6 in)*
This is the militia company of Captain Frans Banning Cocq and Lieutenant Willem van Ruytenburgh. The militia was formed to defend Amsterdam during the Low Countries' war with Spain, and this picture was commissioned for their new meeting hall. Each member of the company contributed to the cost of the commission, so Rembrandt was obliged to include them all. Instead of painting a static group portrait, he decided to show the company on parade, to stage the event as if it were a play, and to illuminate the scene with imaginary spotlights. By now the role of the militia had become mainly ceremonial, so the mood of the picture is relaxed rather than military.

REMBRANDT'S "SPOTLIGHTS"

One light shines diagonally from top left onto Captain Cocq and his lieutenant, another picks out the girl in a yellow dress. To highlight these figures was an unorthodox decision, since it meant sacrificing the importance of individual members for the sake of overall dramatic impact. In 1715 the canvas was moved to Amsterdam's town hall and cut to fit its new space. A wide strip was taken from the left, which substantially altered the composition. Originally Captain Cocq had yet to reach centre stage. Now he stands dead centre – anchored to the spot by the diagonals – so the composition is much more static.

The pike creates one of a number of dramatic diagonals

Area of canvas removed in 1715

The group at the back emerges from the darkness of an archway and so are painted in muted colours

These people are darker and less distinct than the two men behind the lieutenant, who are painted in warm mid-tones

Captain Cocq creates a dark accent

The lieutenant creates a light accent

This group is in subdued light

Colour and form

COLOUR IS AN ESSENTIAL aspect of composition, and it can be used in numerous ways. Artists such as Paul Delaroche (1797–1856) create the impression of volume by means of tone (light and shade), rather than colour (hue). In *The Execution of Lady Jane Grey*, the queen's shift is painted cream with white in the highlights and grey in the shadows. Changes are in tone, not hue. In effect, the picture is a coloured drawing; take away the colour and the volume would remain just as clear. Delaroche uses colour for dramatic effect – to highlight the most important elements in the story – and symbolically, to enhance the drama and pull at our heart strings. The queen's pale dress indicates her innocence and virginity. She goes to her death in the manner of a bride. The lieutenant of the Tower is like a father tenderly giving away his daughter at her wedding.

MADONNA OF THE MEADOWS
Raphael; 1505; 113 x 87 cm (44½ x 34¼ in)
In this serene painting Raphael uses colour in two different ways. In the background the colour creates the illusion of depth. The transition from soft greens to limpid blues creates the impression of a landscape receding into a distant haze. The transition happens rather abruptly at the edge of the lake. Although the landscape is recognizable, here it functions as an idealized backdrop – over which the Madonna is superimposed – rather than an actual scene. The Madonna is a substantial presence – we sense the volume of her body beneath her dress. But the definition of form is achieved more with drawing (tone), than with colour (hue). Here the colour performs a different function; it is symbolic. The red of Mary's dress indicates her humanity, her blue mantle her spirituality. These colours were laid down by the church and were not negotiable.

The Execution of Lady Jane Grey

PAUL DELAROCHE

1833; 246 x 297 cm (8 ft x 9 ft 9 in)

Paul Delaroche is relatively unknown today, but during his lifetime he enjoyed enormous success in the Paris Salon. He specialized in history paintings in which every well-researched detail was rendered with immaculate clarity. Lady Jane Grey, the great-granddaughter of Henry VII, became queen of England for just nine days in 1553, after the death of Edward VII. She was dethroned by Mary I and beheaded in the Tower of London for high treason. Delaroche stages the event as though it were a scene from a play. Not a hair is out of place; everyone is dressed in clean new clothes.

COLOURFUL CHARACTERS
The background is essentially monochrome; the walls are mainly a chill grey. The execution takes place on a wooden platform over which a black cloth has been thrown. Colour is used as a way of highlighting the characters.

SIMPLE SYMBOLISM
Like Raphael, Delaroche uses colour symbolically. His scheme is personal rather than a universally accepted code, but it is obvious and very easy to decipher.

ATMOSPHERIC LIGHTING
Delaroche has bathed the whole scene in a pale light that is chill like morning air. Along with the clarity of the drawing, it creates a sense of cruel indifference.

The executioner wears black (death) and red (blood)

The lieutenant of the Tower helps her to the block

The queen's satin shift accentuates her innocence

COLOURS OF INNOCENCE
The white blindfold indicates the innocence of the young queen, who goes to her death with grace and dignity. Her golden hair falls across her delicate neck, laid bare for the sharp blade. Her jewellery, cap, and gown have been removed to expose her cream satin shift and to emphasize her youth and vulnerability.

A STILL LIFE WITHIN
The stalks of wheat laid under the block to absorb the blood form a delicate still life, symbolizing life cut down in its prime. The ladies in waiting swoon in grief; one bares her neck in a gesture resembling a head laid on the block. With an axe by his side, the executioner looks on, awaiting the job in hand.

Landscape as theatre

IF YOU STAND ON A HILLTOP with a view over a landscape, you will notice that the distant horizon looks bluer and hazier than your immediate surroundings. The atmosphere affects the light passing through it: water vapour and particles of dust absorb the longer, red wavelengths more easily than the shorter, blue ones. This principle, whereby foreground colours appear warmer and distant colours cooler and bluer, is called atmospheric colour. Armed with this knowledge, the French painter Claude Lorrain (1600–82) devised a method for composing landscapes that convincingly depict nature. His understanding of light came from lying in the fields watching the dawn break or the dusk fall and from making detailed sketches of the countryside around Rome, where he lived. He did not translate his drawings directly into paintings, but used them to construct idealized views in which a pale but luminous distance is framed by trees that cast shadows over a dark foreground.

THE CLAUDE GLASS
Invented in the 18th century, a Claude glass is a small convex mirror, backed with silver or black. Painters used its reflection to recreate landscapes with Claude's subtle gradations of colour and tone.

The landscape is framed by the feathery silhouettes of dark trees

A CONTRADICTORY NOTE
Invading this pastoral scene, from the left, is a line of soldiers on horse-back, a reminder that such romantic harmony exists mainly in our dreams.

Landscape with the Marriage of Isaac and Rebekah
CLAUDE LORRAIN *1648; 149 x 197 cm (4 ft 10½ in x 6 ft 5 in)*

Claude constructed his landscapes according to a simple but effective formula. Clumps of trees, to the left and right of the picture, frame the scene like the flats of a stage set. Their feathery mass is silhouetted against a radiant sky. The foreground is dark so that the viewer's attention is drawn towards the light and promise of the distance. In this painting, the boats on the sparkling river take the eye on a zigzag journey back through illusionary space – from the mill on the left bank, across the weir to the town on the other side, coming to rest on the misty hills in the far distance. Besides moving from dark to light, the journey goes from intense foreground colour, through subtle tonal gradations, to a pale wash.

CLAUDE'S COLOURS

Instead of relying on the simple contrast of warm and cool colours – warm browns for the foreground, blues to suggest distance – used by earlier painters of "atmospheric perspective" Claude employed a much subtler range of colours. He alternated bands of warm and cool, from earthy browns and ochres, through greens and soft orange-browns, to a pale, washed-out haze bathed in sunlight.

CLAUDE'S TECHNIQUE

Claude's tonal gradations and limpid light obsessed landscape painters for the next hundred years. Trying to analyze Claude's technique, Turner concluded that he must have painted the tonal gradations in flat colour before adding any people, objects, or other local detail.

Visible picture surface

3

2

1

Background

Vanishing point

Middleground

Foreground

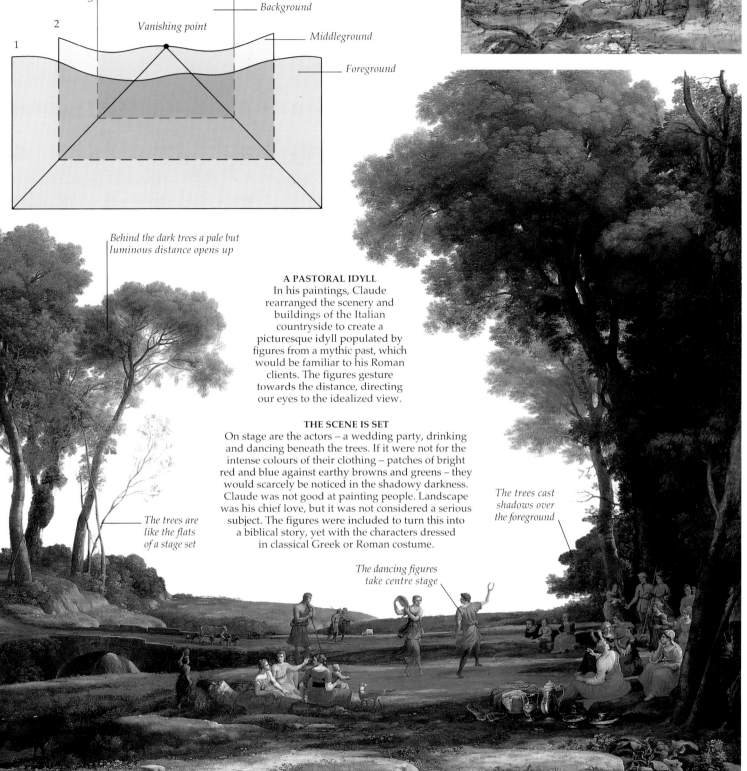

Behind the dark trees a pale but luminous distance opens up

A PASTORAL IDYLL

In his paintings, Claude rearranged the scenery and buildings of the Italian countryside to create a picturesque idyll populated by figures from a mythic past, which would be familiar to his Roman clients. The figures gesture towards the distance, directing our eyes to the idealized view.

THE SCENE IS SET

On stage are the actors – a wedding party, drinking and dancing beneath the trees. If it were not for the intense colours of their clothing – patches of bright red and blue against earthy browns and greens – they would scarcely be noticed in the shadowy darkness. Claude was not good at painting people. Landscape was his chief love, but it was not considered a serious subject. The figures were included to turn this into a biblical story, yet with the characters dressed in classical Greek or Roman costume.

The trees are like the flats of a stage set

The trees cast shadows over the foreground

The dancing figures take centre stage

Composing with light

ROUEN CATHEDRAL
Monet owned this photograph of Rouen Cathedral. In his paintings the solid structure seems to dissolve in the light.

T HE BASIC PRINCIPLE that warm colours – reds, oranges, and yellows – seem to come toward you and cool ones – blues and greens – seem to recede, allows painters to organize their pictures and to create an impression of depth simply by means of colour. During the Victorian era scientists began to understand the relationship between light, colour, and visual perception. At the same time photography (pp. 52–53) – the record of light and shade – was becoming popular. So it is not surprising that artists such as Claude Monet (1840–1926) became interested in similar issues. In his famous series of paintings of Rouen Cathedral, Monet uses the warm/cold colour contrast to evoke the complicated relief of the facade. He also responded to the constantly changing light. The colour of an object and its shadow are strongly affected by the light, so their appearance changes according to the seasons, the weather, and the time of day.

Rouen Cathedral Series

CLAUDE MONET *1892–97*
Monet worked on up to 14 canvases at once, switching as the light changed. In effect, he was trying to be like a camera: recording light and shade. Warm sunshine gives the stone an orange glow; the early morning light, a blue chill. Monet portrayed the building as a light-reflecting screen, so one forgets that this is an ancient structure and thinks instead of the light and temperature of the moment.

ROUEN CATHEDRAL: EFFECT OF THE SUN, END OF THE DAY
Claude Monet; 1892–93;
100 x 65 cm (39¼ x 25½ in)

ROUEN CATHEDRAL: THE PORTAL AND THE TOWER OF SAINT-ROMAIN, MORNING EFFECT, HARMONY IN WHITE
Claude Monet; 1892–94; 106 x 75 cm (41¾ x 29½ in)

ROUEN CATHEDRAL: FULL SUNLIGHT, HARMONY IN BLUE AND GOLD
Claude Monet; 1894;
107 x 73 cm (42 x 28¼ in)

Although Monet is renowned for his oil colour sketches, he made many pencil drawings as an *aide memoire*.

A selection of Monet's portable sketchbooks

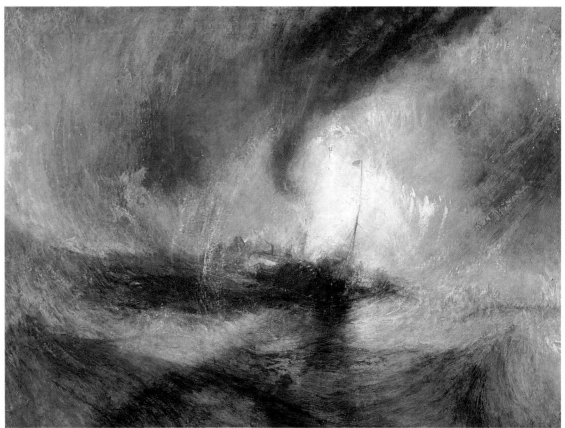

MONET'S SKETCHES

For two months from February 1892 Monet rented a room opposite Rouen Cathedral, enabling him to work from early morning till sunset. He returned at the same time the following year when the light and weather would be similar. He continued to work on the paintings back in Giverny, using the sketches he made on the spot to refresh his memory. Their main function, though, was exploratory: "Each day", he wrote, "I discovered something that I hadn't seen the day before".

SNOWSTORM – STEAMBOAT OFF A HARBOUR'S MOUTH

Joseph Mallord William Turner; 1842; 91.5 x 121.9 cm (36 x 48 in)

Rather than portraying objects in sharp focus, the English landscape painter J.M.W. Turner concentrated on the medium that makes things visible – on light and air. A ship is caught in a fierce storm and Turner's composition is a dramatic vortex spiralling round the vessel, dimly visible in the driving rain. Everything solid has dissolved into the seething maelstrom of the elements. To experience the event fully, Turner had himself lashed to the mast of a ship during a storm.

ROUEN CATHEDRAL: MORNING SUN, HARMONY IN BLUE
Claude Monet; 1894;
91 x 63 cm (35¼ x 24¾ in)

ROUEN CATHEDRAL: THE PORTAL, GREY WEATHER
Claude Monet; 1894;
100 x 65 cm (39¼ x 25½ in)

ROUEN CATHEDRAL: THE PORTAL SEEN FROM THE FRONT, HARMONY IN BROWN
Claude Monet; 1894;
107 x 73 cm (42 x 28¼ in)

Pure colour

COLOUR HAS COME into its own in the 20th century. Synthetic pigments have made available such a vast range of striking colours that artists can treat hue as an element in its own right, independent of form. Fauvists such as Henri Matisse composed their paintings entirely in terms of colour. Although *Portrait of Madame Matisse* is a recognizable portrait, it is primarily a vibrant study in colour contrast. Divided into areas of green, red, purple, Prussian blue, ochre, and pink, the abstract design is as important to the composition as the head it portrays. Other artists went even further and took the plunge into pure abstraction; Yves Klein's (1928–1962) monochromes are the most extreme form of abstraction. In these works colour seems to have no boundaries and pulsates off the canvas to envelop the viewer.

IKB 79
Yves Klein; 1959; 139.7 x 119.7 x 3.2 cm (55 x 47 x 1¼ in); acrylic, fabric and wood
Yves Klein was a member of the religious sect, the Rosicrucians. He developed his monochrome blue paintings as the embodiment of "the cosmic energy of pure colour". His ambition was to provide a spiritual experience, and he chose blue because of its long association with spirituality in Christian art. He developed an intense hue from a secret recipe and named it International Klein Blue (IKB). The paint is applied uniformly so there are no visible brushmarks or variations in texture to draw attention to the surface. Numerous layers build up an astonishing vibrance so that the colour seems to dematerialize and shimmer off the surface.

RAIN
Howard Hodgkin; 1985–89; 163.8 x 179 cm (5 ft 4 in x 5 ft 9 in); oil on wood
Blue is also important in this painting by Howard Hodgkin (born 1932). The blue brushstroke breaks through the oppressive grey bands framing the central area of colour. The image is like a view through a window onto a landscape dark with clouds. The blue swish suggests a curtain blowing in the wind. Hodgkin's paintings are based on actual events – a dinner party, a conversation – and begin life quite realistically. Then, over a long period, the experience is abstracted to the point where form and colour are like recollections, evoking the mood of the remembered occasion.

Portrait of Madame Matisse

HENRI MATISSE *1905; 40.6 x 32.4 cm (16 x 12¾ in)*
In this revolutionary painting Matisse shows how
colour, rather than tone, can create volume. Recent
experiments in colour photography (pp. 52–53) had
shown that all the colours of the spectrum could
be created by mixing red, green and blue light. A
photograph gives an impression of volume simply
by recording light. Here Matisse does a similar thing
in paint: he creates an image using blocks of colour
rather than line and tone.

Cadmium
Yellow

Ultramarine
blue

Vermillion

Using photography

THE CAMERA OBSCURA was popular with artists as long ago as the 16th century. A lens projected the view onto a mirror, which reflected it onto a sheet of paper. The image could then be traced and used as the basis for a painting. Few artists admitted using them, but even the renowned Canaletto (1697–1768) relied on a portable "dark room" to map out his crystal clear paintings of Venice. When ways of fixing the image with chemicals were announced in Paris in 1839, the news caused a furore. "From today painting is dead", exclaimed Paul Delaroche (pp. 44–45) when he saw his first photograph. Nicknamed "the school of the eyes", the French Impressionists behaved as though they were cameras by trying to capture the quality of a single moment in paint; Edgar Degas (1834–1917) took his own photographs and owed his radical ideas for compositions to photography.

BOULEVARD DE STRASBOURG
Hippolyte Jouvin; 1860–65; stereoscopic photograph
Jouvin's views of busy Paris streets sold in vast numbers. The prints were mainly stereoscopic, taken from two slightly different viewpoints to mimic sight so that, when viewed in a stereoscope, the scene appeared three-dimensional. Jouvin's unusual viewpoints, achieved by shooting from an upper window, reduced people to odd little silhouettes. For the first time city life was seen as an arbitrary bustle of activity, a continually changing pattern of movement, and the individual as an anonymous member of the crowd.

EARLY PHOTOGRAPHY
Even though the camera was an extension of the camera obscura, the invention of photography – of ways of fixing the image with salts – had a dramatic impact on the way artists saw, and therefore composed, their paintings. Early techniques required such long exposures that anything that moved appeared as a blur in the final image. But by 1858 exposures of only 1/50th of a second were possible, which allowed artists to record street scenes.

BOULEVARD MONTMARTRE: RAINY WEATHER, AFTERNOON
Camille Pissarro; 1897; 52.5 x 66 cm (20¾ x 26 in)
In 1897 Camille Pissarro (1831–1903) rented a room in Paris, which gave him a view down the Boulevard Montmartre. Over the next two months he painted 14 pictures of the boulevard, "almost as the crow flies, looking over the carriages, buses, and people milling about between the large trees and big houses". He painted the street as a canyon fringed by trees and buildings, rapidly receding into the distance. The high viewpoint transforms people and vehicles into indistinct shapes, a pattern of dark blobs against a lighter ground. This type of composition, completely new in painting, owed its origins to photographs like those taken by Hippolyte Jouvin (above).

LA-LA AT THE CIRQUE FERNANDO
Edgar Degas; 1879; 116.8 x 77.5 cm (46 x 30½ in)
"No artist would have dared to draw a walking figure in attitudes like some of these", was one response to "instantaneous photographs", which froze action and made it possible to see the positions taken up by bodies in motion. Degas was fascinated; his friend Ernest Rouart remarked the he "loved and appreciated photography at a time when other artists despised it". This painting of a circus performer was based on sketches, but the odd viewpoint and the idea of recording the twirling figure hanging by her teeth were inspired by photography.

DANCERS IN THE WINGS
Edgar Degas; c.1886; 69.5 x 50 cm (27¼ x 19¾ in); pastel and tempera on paper
Some of Degas's pictures can be traced to specific photographs. An 1860 sketch of two dancers in crinolines is based on a photograph by André Disderi, who specialized in photographing ballerinas. The strange composition of this pastel obviously borrows its apparently random framing from photographs; you feel sure that, at any moment, the camera will pan right to centre the dancers.

DEGAS THE PHOTOGRAPHER
Degas collected and took photographs like this one as source material for paintings that were very different from other Impressionists' works. He painted his subjects from unusual angles and viewpoints, in strange poses, positioned oddly within the space, or cut off by the frame – all "slice of life" approaches to composition typical of photography, but never before seen in painting.

Depicting motion

BEFORE THE INVENTION of photography, artists like Jacques-Louis David (1748–1825) had difficulty portraying movement on the static two-dimensional surface of the canvas. They had to rely on rapid sketching to achieve a convincing likeness of a body caught mid-action. But our vision is too slow to perceive the positions of a moving body, so models were posed as though walking, running, and so on. Since a horse could not be persuaded to fake a gallop, artists had to rely on guesswork. In 1887 the English photographer Eadweard Muybridge published a set of sequential photographs of a walking woman, jumping man, and galloping horse taken with batteries of cameras whose shutters were triggered by trip wires. They were a revelation, proving that the popular "flying gallop", with all four legs spread out, was quite wrong. Whereas a photograph freezes a split second, a chronophotograph records a movement developing through time and space. Its introduction in 1882 gave artists yet another new source of material to work with.

SWIFTS: PATHS OF MOVEMENT AND DYNAMIC SEQUENCES
Giacomo Balla; 1913; 96.8 x 120 cm (38 x 47¼ in)
The Italian Futurists (p. 62) were determined to bring art into the 20th century and to respond to the exciting inventions of the time – the telephone, radio, motor car, electricity, and motion picture – with forms that embodied the energy and speed of the era. "We declare", they announced in 1909, "that the world's splendour has been enriched by a new beauty: the beauty of speed". Flight embodied all the things they admired. Balla (1871–1958) was a key member of the group; his painting closely follows Marey's photographs and diagrams of a bird in flight (above, right).

Napoleon Crossing the Alps

JACQUES-LOUIS DAVID *1801; 245.5 x 231.5 cm (8 ft x 7 ft 7¼ in)*
As the most celebrated artist in France at the time, Jacques-Louis David was commissioned to glorify Napoleon's crossing of the Alps to conquer northern Italy. The First Consul actually went on a mule in fine weather but, in order to add dynamism to the composition, David invented a storm to frighten the horse and to blow his mane and tail (and Napoleon's cloak) in the direction of the advance. David copied the rearing horse from a sculpture, and his son perched on a ladder in an attempt to capture Napoleon's dramatic pose. Not surprisingly, the results are rather unconvincing.

CHRONOPHOTOGRAPH OF THE FLIGHT OF A BIRD
Étienne-Jules Marey; 1887
Eadweard Muybridge set out to show the exact
positions of a horse's legs during the gallop and to
record every conceivable human movement. His
photographs were taken with banks of cameras,
each of which recorded a different phase of the
action with a shutter speed of 1/1000th of a second.
The French physiologist Étienne-Jules Marey,
on the other hand, was more interested in the
abstract patterns and rhythms of movement than
in anatomical changes in the subject. He either left
the shutter of his one camera open or activated it
repeatedly, so as to capture the whole action on a
single plate. This resulted in a chronophotograph
and revealed the continuous flow of a movement
as it unfolded in space and in time.

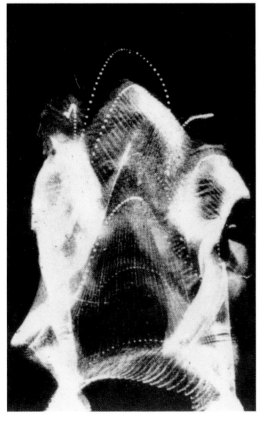

**CHRONOPHOTOGRAPH OF A FIGURE
DURING A STANDING JUMP**
Étienne-Jules Marey; late 19th century
Marey sometimes attached white strips and
bright spots to the arms, legs and hands of people
dressed in black and moving in front of black
screens. The photographs recording these actions
resemble diagrams or abstract drawings, and from
them Marey made graphs analyzing patterns of
movement. Rather than dissecting motion into its
constituent parts, Marey emphasizes the continuity
of forms as they move laterally through time.

NUDE DESCENDING A STAIRCASE NO 2
Marcel Duchamp; 1912; 147 x 89 cm (58 x 35 in)
The French artist Marcel Duchamp (1887–1968)
freely admitted that the superimposed images
of his robotic figure spiralling down a staircase
were inspired by Marey's chronophotographs.
The dotted curves and lines that chart the
rhythm, flow, and direction of the robot's
movements are also borrowed from Marey's
photographs and diagrams. Duchamp was
eager to invent forms that reflected the
dynamism of the new machine age.

Double images

THINGS ARE NOT ALWAYS always what
they seem. Double images give more
than one set of information and work
by associating one thing with another.
Giuseppe Arcimboldo (1527–93) creates
one shape (a head) out of a multitude
of others (sea creatures). Rationally the
image makes no sense, but the shapes are
so carefully overlaid – a shell for an ear,
say – that the matching seems plausible.
The objects in Salvador Dali's (1904–89)
paintings often seem to change before
your eyes. In *Metamorphosis of Narcissus* a
rock, a boy, and a hand all have the same
form, as though mysteriously connected.
Hannah Höch (1889–1978) pasted together
segments of photographs to suggest a
discrepancy between appearances and
other levels of feeling and experience.

*Narcissus glows golden
like warm rock in the
setting sun; he appears
radiant with
self-love*

*His hair is like a cleft
in the rocks behind, as
though he were part of
the landscape*

*The knee
becomes the
third finger
of the bony
hand*

WATER
*Giuseppe Arcimboldo;
1566; 67 x 52 cm (26⅛ x
20½ in); oil on limewood*
Giuseppe Arcimboldo
specialized in heads
made up of flowers,
fruit or landscapes.
This fish portrait
is of the Hapsburg
Emperor, Maximilian
II. The mouth is a
shark, the cheek a ray,
the eyebrow a squilla,
and so on. The scale of
the creatures is dictated
by the head rather than
their actual size, so a
shrimp becomes as big
as a shark. The results
may seem grotesque,
but the portraits were
intended as flattery.

Metamorphosis of Narcissus

SALVADOR DALI *1937; 50.8 x 78.2 cm (20 x 30¼ in)*
According to Greek myth, Narcissus fell in love with his reflection in a pool, was unable to drag himself away, and died. He was then transformed into a flower. Dali paints Narcissus in the landscape of northern Spain, as though he were a rock that has weathered into the shape of a figure. On the shore a bony hand represents Fate, its form mimicking that of the boy: his knee becomes a thumbnail, his upper arm a finger, his head an egg-shaped bulb and flower. Spaniards refer to neurosis as "a bulb in the head" and such extreme self-obsession is regarded as neurotic.

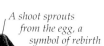

SALVADOR DALI
Dali was a member of the French Surrealists, who were influenced by Sigmund Freud, the father of psychoanalysis, and his idea of the unconscious as a pool of hidden thoughts and feelings.

Narcissi flower in early spring; the egg-shaped bulb refers to rebirth and the cycle of life and death

A shoot sprouts from the egg, a symbol of rebirth

The fingers are like bone, as though this were the hand of death. Ants run up the thumb, suggesting great age or putrefaction

DA-DANDY
Hannah Höch; 1919; 30 x 23 cm; (11¼ x 9 in); paper collage
Hannah Höch uses collage, cut and pasted photographs, to convey neurosis or the mismatch between inner feeling and outer form. Heads are attached to inappropriate bodies to create schizophrenic monsters. Features from different faces are joined, with no regard to scale, so that they convey conflicting messages. The results are sometimes comical, sometimes frightening. Frenzy and hysteria seem to prevail – a reflection, perhaps, of the mood gripping Berlin, where she began her collages, during World War I.

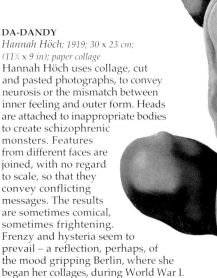

The role of chance

EVERYONE HAS SEEN faces or animals in the clouds, but it may surprise you to discover that Leonardo da Vinci, the grand master of composition (pp. 28–29) advised young artists to draw inspiration from looking "at a wall spotted with stains, ashes on the hearth, or clouds or steam ... you may see battles and figures in action, or strange faces and costumes, or an endless variety of objects". It was not until the 1920s that artists began to look systematically for fresh ways to generate ideas. The father of psychoanalysis, Sigmund Freud, discovered the unconscious mind, as revealed to us in our dreams, to be a treasure house of imaginative fantasy. But how is it possible to gain access to the unconscious when you are awake and reason is in control? Inspired by Freud, the Surrealists devised a range of techniques, many using chance, to generate images that were not predetermined. Max Ernst (1891–1976) described this as "attending as a spectator the birth of all my works".

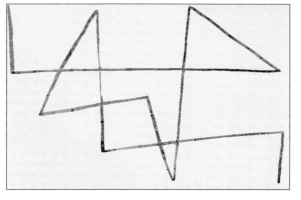

THE WAY OUT AT LAST
Paul Klee; 1935; 32 x 48 cm (12⅝ x 18⅞ in); watercolour on paper
The Swiss artist Paul Klee (1879–1940) described his method of drawing as "taking a line for a walk". Journeys and paths often feature in his work; they serve as metaphors for his interest in the creative process rather than the end product. "Never work towards a ready-made pictorial impression", he advised. "Do not think of form but of formation." Klee taught at the Bauhaus, the famous German art school. In 1925 the school published his *Pedagogical Sketchbook*, a detailed handbook on composition that demonstrated his mystical belief in the links between things on a cosmic and a microscopic scale.

THE ROVING LINE
Klee's drawings are often made with a single continuous line that turns back on itself in squares or zigzags to create the impression of a village, a forest, sailing boats or, as here, a maze-like succession of transparent planes within which a family is trapped. The line begins as an abstract pattern created spontaneously. Elements such as the figures are then added. Klee's work may look childlike, but this comes from a desire to strip away appearances and reveal the laws governing the structure of all things.

USING THE TEXTURE
In this painting Ernst used his technique of *decalcomania*: spreading paint onto a textured surface, pressing canvas against it, then peeling it off. Here he also took rubbings from planks and pressed textured objects against the wet paint.

PRECONCEIVED COMPOSITION
The initial idea was arrived at through chance, but the painting is extremely carefully composed. The wooden planks, placed to create the impression of a dead forest, the lunar disc, and the small bird scratched into the paint on the right, are all carefully planned.

IMAGES FROM BEYOND
The Surrealists believed that by using chance they were dredging images up from the unconscious. "Before he goes into the water, a diver cannot know what he will bring back", Ernst said of starting a picture with no preconceived ideas.

WAS IT REALLY CHANCE?
To a certain extent the Surrealists were deluding themselves. The imprint or rubbing was just a beginning. Having attained an area of texture, Ernst still had to make it into art. He made eight similar paintings, so suggesting a good deal of planning.

View of the Port of St. Denis

MAX ERNST *1927; 114.5 x 146.5 cm (45 x 57¼ in)*

The German Surrealist Max Ernst devised numerous ways of generating ideas. One was *frottage*. In 1925, while staying in a seaside hotel, he noticed the deep grain of the scrubbed floorboards. Using black crayon he began making rubbings, transferring the pattern of the woodgrain to sheets of paper to produce "a hallucinatory succession of contradictory images". Additions and modifications turned these into drawings of animals, plants, and landscapes. Other techniques included *collage*, juxtaposing fragments of images from diverse sources, and *decalcomania* (p. 62), used to create this image.

MAX ERNST
When asked as a child what was his favourite pastime, Ernst replied, "Looking". His fascination with woodgrain began when he was ill. A temperature caused him to hallucinate and see faces in a mahogany panel at the end of his bed. His later *frottages* were like artificially induced hallucinations. He frequently used a mixture of techniques in one work.

Breaking the frame

I<small>N</small> 1912 P<small>ABLO</small> P<small>ICASSO</small> (1881–1973) made his first relief assemblage, a guitar made from scraps of metal. Instead of describing the surface of the object, he took it apart and reconstructed it. The skin of illusion (of painting) had been dismantled and replaced by an accumulation of fragments that occupy real rather than imaginary space and lead a double life: as recognizable bits and pieces (card, wood, metal, and so on) and as representations. While some artists have continued to paint, others explore the relationship between painting and sculpture. The elements of Frank Stella's abstract composition act as independent agents; they seem to have gelled in an orderly fashion only for the time being. Look away and the whole configuration might have rearranged itself. But even when the parts are off the wall, as in the painted reliefs of the young English artist Julian Opie, the laws of composition still apply. Balance, proportion, scale, interval, and so on are still vital. Picasso's *Still Life* may be rebellious, but it is a superbly balanced composition.

Guitars were a favourite subject of Picasso's. He made paintings and assemblages of them from bits of metal and card. They signify both "painting" and "sculpture"

This strip of wood evokes a dado and a picture frame

This board is like the café wall and the picture plane

The objects are made of painted steel

This French meal is a tribute to Picasso, Braque, and Cubism

Still Life

PABLO PICASSO; 1914; 25.4 x 45.7 x 9.2 cm
(10 x 18 x 3¾ in); wood, tassle
Still life was a favourite theme for Picasso, a way of evoking the café society of Paris. He made this playful still life from odd scraps of wood and a piece of upholstery fringe. The assemblage is an exploration into the nature of representation. At the back is a piece of wood that refers to two things: to the wall of the café against which the semi-circular table rests, and to what would be the surface if this were a painting. The horizontal strip of dark wood similarly refers to the dado of the café wall and the frame of the "picture". The upholstery fringe represents a tablecloth while also retaining its own abstract identity. The glass, the knife and the slice of bread are also part way between real objects and pictorial representations. Neither a painting nor a sculpture, the work derives its wit from the ambiguity of being both an image and an object.

STELLER'S ALBATROSS (#6, 5.5X)
Frank Stella; 1976; 305 x 419 cm (10 ft x 13 ft 9 in);
mixed media on aluminium
In the 1960s Frank Stella made rigidly geometric
paintings in which the shape of the canvas
dictated the stark arrangement of lines within
its borders. These compositions, made up of
black stripes or bands of plain colour, insistently
repeated the shape established by the edges,
so that a square canvas gave rise to a nest of
squares, a lozenge to diagonal stripes. Then
in the 1970s, as though in a daring burst of
rebellious energy, the shapes took on a life of
their own, leapt off the canvas, and began to
prance about the wall. Now made of honeycomb
aluminium, they are independent of each other.

*All the shapes are
cut out of sheet steel,
which is flat, and
painted to look round*

*This painted sculpture
pays homage to
Picasso's first
assemblage*

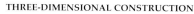

THREE-DIMENSIONAL CONSTRUCTION
Strips, arabesques, and French curves are
soldered onto a backing grid. Onto the
shapes are painted swirls, squiggles,
blobs, and daubs in a gaudy variety
of colours, as though someone had
been experimenting with spray-can
graffiti. Each shape is painted separately,
determined to assert its independence
from the pack. The resulting cacophony
is a joyous romp out of the picture frame.
The shapes seem to lean, tilt and slide,
but Stella does not actually take them
off the wall. These objects still cling to
the idea that they are part of the history
of painting and may choose, one day,
to return sedately to the frame.

DÉJEUNER SUR LE PLANCHER
Julian Opie; 1984; 125 x 110 x 110 cm (49¼ x 43⅓ x 43⅓ in)
The contents of this still life seem to have stepped out of
the frame, toppled off the wall, and landed on the floor
where they have arranged themselves in readiness for
a party. Each object is obviously painted; the garish
colours make no pretence at being naturalistic. The
brushmarks are so crude that they deliberately draw
attention to themselves and their own artifice. How
do these painted enigmas stand up? Each item is cut
out of steel, then painted to look like an illusion. The
sculpture masquerades as a painting; it occupies real
space, but it is only to be looked at from the front.

A CASUAL DEPICTION
The painting is so perfunctory that it is more like
a depiction of a painting than an attempt at realism –
a representation of a representation rather than the
illusion of an object. The label on the bottle is painted
so sketchily that it looks like a close-up analysis of an
artist's paint handling, showing how the impression
was created magically, with a few swishes of
the brush. Opie is playing a double game. While
apparently making no attempt to fool the viewer
with a realistic image, instead he fools you into
thinking that these cut-outs are painted illusions.
The subject is the relationship between painting
and sculpture and the nature of representation itself.

Glossary

Abstraction A term that can be employed to describe any art that does not represent recognizable objects. In the 20th century, it has been applied to works in which colour and form convey ideas or evoke feelings.

Allegory A picture in which the characters or events are used to symbolize a moral or spiritual theme.

Asymmetry see **symmetry**

Atmospheric perspective Particles in the earth's atmosphere absorb and scatter light. The red end is affected more than the blue end. Artists mimic this effect by using blue, hazier tones towards the horizon.

Detail of Claude's *use of atmospheric perspective*

Background The space behind the figures in a picture.

Complementary colours The complementary of a **primary colour** is achieved by mixing the two other primaries. The complementary of red is green, of yellow purple, and of blue orange. Placed next to each other, both appear more vibrant. Optically they are triggered by one another. Stare at a bright yellow light or object and everything else seems tinged with purple.

Composition The considered arrangement of the various parts of a work of art.

Cool colours Colours that tend towards blue, most obviously those in the blue-green-violet range. In a painting, cool colours appear to recede.

Curvilinear A composition dominated by circles or rounded, flowing lines.

Decalcomania Technique developed by Max Ernst whereby paint is spread onto a textured surface, canvas pressed against it, then peeled off.

Diagonal A diagonal line or plane, often joining points in opposite corners of the canvas.

Ellipse Closed conic section shaped like a flattened circle and formed by an inclined plane that does not cut the base of the cone.

Equilateral triangle A triangle with sides of equal length. Used as the compositional shape for some paintings, particularly those with a Christian theme as the triangle represents the Holy **Trinity**.

Fauvism The name *Les Fauves* (The Wild Beasts) was applied by a hostile critic to artists such as Matisse, who exhibited at the Salon d'Automne in Paris in 1905. Characteristics of Fauvism are brilliant colour, abstract shapes, and distortions of figurative forms.

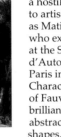

Foreground The part of a picture nearest to the viewer.

Foreshortening Drawing an object so that the parts appear to diminish as they recede into the distance.

Frottage (French: "rubbing") Technique whereby paper is placed over a rough surface such as wood, coins, or engraved brass, and rubbed with pencil or charcoal until the texture is reproduced on the paper.

Futurism Italian art movement founded in 1909 that also incorporated poetry, architecture, music, and photography. Aim was to break with the past and to celebrate modern technology and dynamism. Depiction of movement was a key concern for artists.

Piero's use of sacred geometry

Golden Section / Golden Ratio A proportion, discovered in Ancient Greece, whereby a straight line is divided into two unequal parts in such a way that the ratio of the smaller to the greater part is the same as that of the greater to the whole (a line AB divided at C so that AB:AC=AC:BC). A rectangle constructed to Golden Section proportions can be further divided to create a spiral. Considered by some to be divine, the proportion is found in the structure of various plants and shells.

Horizon line In nature this is the line where sea and sky appear to meet. In a painting the horizon line is an imaginary line drawn across the **picture plane** at the viewer's eye level.

Hue The apparent colour of a visual sensation, described as "red", "blue", and so on.

Linear perspective A system of drawing based on the fact that objects appear to get smaller, and parallel lines to converge, with distance. Can be applied to both vertical and horizontal lines.

Middle ground The picture plane between the **foreground** and the **background**.

Minimalism The use of simple geometric forms in art.

Naturalism Art that represents objects as they are observed.

Orthogonals Lines that gradually converge to meet at the **vanishing point** and represent lines at right angles to the **picture plane** receding into depth. They draw the viewer's eye into depth.

Perspective Method of representing the illusion of spatial recession on a flat surface.

Picture plane The flat surface on which a picture is painted. This vertical plane is imagined as a window pane between the viewer (or artist) and the scene depicted.

Primary colours These are the three colours – red, blue, yellow – from which all others are derived. They cannot be created by mixture, but can be combined to create other colours.

Proportion Similar to the idea of ratio, this is the comparison of two things of the same kind. Also the relationship between

any part and the whole of an object or length.

Rectangle The most common shape of a canvas and also the most flexible. Described as "landscape" if horizontal and "portrait" if vertical.

Sacred geometry The belief by certain Italian Renaissance artists that everything in the universe was ordered according to a divine set of mathematic principles. See also **Golden Section / Golden Ratio**.

Manet's *use of a vertical pose*

Secondary colours A colour made by mixing two primaries together.

Steelyard A weighing machine with a short arm for the object being weighed and a long arm on which a single weight moves.

Surrealism Art that represents an exploration of the irrational and subconscious. Surrealist artists included Salvador Dali and Max Ernst .

Symmetry Beauty or harmony of form based on a proportionate arrangement of parts. Perfect symmetry is where one half of a painting mirrors the other exactly. Asymmetry is where two halves of a picture are obviously different.

Rembrandt's use of tonal composition

Tone Lightness or darkness of a colour measured against a scale from black to white.

Trinity The Christian belief in a triple entity of God the Father, God the Son, and the Holy Spirit in one Godhead.

Vanishing point In paintings using **linear perspective**, the point on the horizon at which converging lines meet.

Warm colours Colours that tend towards red, most obviously those in the red-orange-yellow range. In a painting, warm colours appear to advance.

Featured works

Look here to find the location of, and complete details about, the works featured in this book.

This section also includes photographic acknowledgements, although further information can be found under "Acknowledgements" (p. 64)

Every effort has been made to trace the copyright holders and we apologize in advance for any unintentional omissions. We would be pleased to insert the appropriate acknowledgement in any subsequent edition of this publication.

Key: *t:* top *b:* bottom *c:* centre *l:* left *r:* right

Abbreviations:
AKG: Archiv für Kunst und Geschichte, Berlin; **KHM:** Kunsthistorisches Museum, Vienna; **MM:** Musée Marmottan, Paris; **NGL:** Reproduced by courtesy of the Trustees of the National Gallery, London; **OKB:** Oeffentliche Kunstsammlung, Basel, Kunstmuseum; **SC:** Scala; **TG:** Tate Gallery, London

Raphael's *Madonna of the Chairs*

Front cover (clockwise from top right): *Horse Attacked by a Lion*, George Stubbs, TG; *Youth of Moses (detail)*, Sandro Botticelli, Sistine Chapel/SC; *Crucifixion*, Raphael, NGL; *The Avenue, Middelharnis*, Meindert Hobbema, NGL; *Madonna della Sedia*, Raphael, Galleria Palatina, Florence/SC; *Portrait of Victorine Meurent*, Edouard Manet, Gift of Richard C. Paine in memory of his father, Robert Treat Paine II, courtesy of Museum of Fine Arts, Boston; *Prometheus Bound (detail)*, Peter Paul Rubens, Philadelphia Museum of Art: The W. P. Wilstach Collection; *centre: The Artist in his Studio (Allegorie der Malerei)*, Jan Vermeer, KHM. **Back cover (clockwise from top left):** *Parable of the Blind*, Pieter Breughel the Elder, Museo di Capodimonte, Naples/SC; *Self-Portrait*, Rembrandt van Rijn, English Heritage Photographic Library; *A Boy Bringing Bread*, Pieter de Hooch, Reproduced by permission of the Trustees of the Wallace Collection; *The Night Watch*, Rembrandt van Rijn, Rijksmuseum, Amsterdam; *The Baptism of Christ*, Piero della Francesca, NGL; *The Family of Darius Before Alexander*, Paolo Veronese, NGL; *centre: Landscape with the Marriage of Isaac and Rebekah ("The Mill")*, Claude, NGL. **Inside front flap:** *t: "The Rokeby Venus"*, Velázquez, NGL; *b: Rouen Cathedral: Full Sunlight, Harmony in Blue and Gold*, Monet, MM. **p1:** *The Rape of the Daughters of Leucippus*, Peter Paul Rubens, Alte

Pinakothek, Munich/SC. **p2:** *tl: The Family of Darius Before Alexander*, Paolo Veronese, NGL; *tr: The Virgin and Child with Saints George and Anthony Abbot (detail)*, Antonio Pisanello, NGL; *cl: Self-Portrait*, Rembrandt van Rijn, English Heritage Photographic Library; *c: The Rape of the Daughters of Leucippus*, Peter Paul Rubens, Alte Pinakothek, Munich/SC. **pp2–3:** *The Family of Darius Before Alexander*, Paolo Veronese, NGL. **p3:** *tc: The Artist in his Studio (Allegorie der Malerei)*, Jan Vermeer, KHM; *br: Nude Girl*, Gwen John, TG. **p4:** *tl: Vitruvian Man*, Leonardo da Vinci, Galleria dell'Accademia, Venice/AKG; *tr: Parable of the Blind*, Pieter Breughel the Elder, Museo di Capodimonte, Naples/SC; *cl (top): Degas-type camera*, Musée Français de la photographie, Bièvres; *cr (top): Madonna della Sedia*, Raphael, Galleria Palatina, Florence/SC; *cl (bottom): Snapshot*, Edgar Degas, Bibliothèque Nationale, Paris; *cr (bottom): Prometheus Bound (detail)*, Peter Paul Rubens, Philadelphia Museum of Art: The W. P. Wilstach Collection; *b: The Body of the Dead Christ in the Tomb*, Hans Holbein the Younger, OKB, photo: Martin Bühler. **p5:** *The Avenue, Middelharnis*, Meindert Hobbema, NGL

Pages 6–7 Composing a picture
p6: *cl: Guitar Player*, Edouard Manet, Hill-Stead Museum, Farmington, CT 06032; *b: Portrait of Victorine Meurent*, Manet, Gift of Richard C. Paine in memory of his father, Robert Treat Paine II, courtesy of Museum of Fine Arts, Boston. **pp6–7:** *Gare Saint-Lazare*, Gift of Horace Havemeyer in memory of his mother, Louisse W. Havemeyer, © 1995 Board of Trustees, National Gallery of Art, Washington. **p7:** *cr: The Street Singer*, Manet, Bequest of Sarah Choate Sears in memory of her husband, Joshua Montgomery Sears, courtesy of Museum of Fine Arts, Boston; *b: Le Déjeuner sur l'Herbe*, Manet, Musée d'Orsay

Pages 8–9 Canvas shape
p8: *l: Self-Portrait*, Rembrandt van Rijn, English Heritage Photographic Library. **pp8–9:** *An Autumn Landscape with a View of "Het Steen", in the Early Morning*, Peter Paul Rubens, NGL. **p9:** *tr: Nude Girl*, Gwen John, TG; *b: The Body of the Dead Christ in the Tomb*, Hans Holbein the Younger, OKB, photo: Martin Bühler

Pages 10–11 Leading the eye
pp10–11: *A Boy Bringing Bread*, Pieter de Hooch, Reproduced by permission of the Trustees of the Wallace Collection

Pages 12–13 Placing the figure
p12: *t & cr: Portrait of Victorine Meurent*, Edouard Manet, Gift of Richard C. Paine in memory of his father, Robert Treat Paine II, courtesy of Museum of Fine Arts, Boston; *bl: Oi Yoi Yoi*, Roger Hilton, TG, © Estate of Roger Hilton 1995, All rights reserved DACS. **p13:** *Self-Portrait*, Vincent van Gogh, Musée d'Orsay, Paris.

Pages 14–15 Symmetry/asymmetry
p14: *The Virgin and Child with Saints George and Anthony Abbot*, Antonio Pisanello, NGL. **pp14–15:** *Mr and Mrs Andrews*, Thomas Gainsborough, NGL

Pages 16–17 Sacred geometry
p16: *The Baptism of Christ*, Piero della Francesca, NGL. **p17:** *Crucifixion*, Raphael, NGL

Pages 18–19 Triangular designs
p18: *Madonna of the Meadows*, Raphael, KHM. **p19:** *tl: Crucifixion*, Raphael, NGL; *tr, b: The Large Bathers*, Paul Cézanne, Philadelphia Museum of Art, Purchased: W. P. Wilstach

Pages 20–21 Curvilinear compositions
p20: *The Rape of the Daughters of Leucippus*, Peter Paul Rubens, Alte Pinakothek, Munich/SC. **p21:** *The Origin of the Milky Way*, Jacopo Tintoretto, NGL

Pages 22–23 Dramatic diagonals
p22: *Prometheus Bound*, Peter Paul Rubens, Philadelphia Museum of Art: The W. P. Wilstach Collection. **p23:** *The Last Supper*, Jacopo Tintoretto, Lucca, Duomo/SC

Pages 24–25 Shaped paintings
p24: *t: Crucifix*, Style of Segna di Bonaventura, NGL; *bl, br: Madonna of the Chair*, Raphael, Galleria Palatina, Florence/SC. **p25:** *Horse Attacked by a Lion*, George Stubbs, TG; *br: Targowica III*, Frank Stella, Bridgeman Art Library/© ARS, NY and DACS, London 1995

Pages 26–27 The Horizon
p26: *cl: Herdsman with Cows by a River*, Aelbert Cuyp, NGL; *bc: Sketch for Hadleigh Castle*, John Constable, TG

Pages 28–29 The vanishing point
p28: *The Last Supper*, Leonardo da Vinci, Santa Maria della Grazie, Milan/Alinari-Giraudon. **p29:** *The Avenue, Middelharnis*, Meindert Hobbema, NGL

Pages 30–31 Moving the horizon
p30: *tr, bl: Saint James Led to Execution*, Andrea Mantegna, Archivi Alinari; *br: Drawing – Saint James Led to Execution*, Mantegna, The Trustees of the British Museum, London. **p31:** *Waterlilies*, Claude Monet, MM

Pages 32–33 Golden Section
p32: *bl,* **p33:** *tr: The Artist in his Studio (Allegorie der Malerei)*, Jan Vermeer, KHM; **p33:** *bl: Vitruvian Man*, Leonardo da Vinci, Galleria dell'Accademia, Venice/AKG

Pages 34–35 Eye-to-eye contact
p34: *l: "The Rokeby Venus" (The Toilet of Venus)*, Diego Velázquez, NGL; *tr: Self-Portrait*, Rembrandt van Rijn, English Heritage Photographic Library. **pp34–35:** *"The Rokeby Venus"*, Velázquez, NGL; **p35:** *tl: "The Rokeby Venus" with Model (photo)*, Velázquez, NGL; *tr: Olympia*, Edouard Manet, Musée d'Orsay

Pages 36–37 Sequence of events
p36: *bl: Noise of the Street Entering the House*, Umberto Boccioni, Sprengel Museum, Hanover/photo: Michael Herling. **pp36–37:** *Youth of Moses*, Sandro Botticelli, Sistine Chapel/SC

Pages 38–39 Depicting an episode
pp38–39: *Parable of the Blind*, Pieter Breughel the Elder, Museo di Capodimonte, Naples/SC

Pages 40–41 Painting as theatre
p40: *tl: The Banquet of Cleopatra*, Giovanni Battista Tiepolo, Palazzo Labia, Venice/AKG. **pp40–41:** *The Family of Darius Before Alexander*, Paolo Veronese, NGL

Pages 42–43 Tonal values
pp42–43: *The Night Watch*, Rembrandt van Rijn, Rijksmuseum, Amsterdam

Pages 44–45 Colour and form
p44: *bl: Madonna of the Meadows*, Raphael, KHM. **pp44–45:** *The Execution of Lady Jane Grey*, Paul Delaroche, NGL

Stubbs' *Horse Attacked by a Lion*

Pages 46–47 Landscape as theatre
p46: *tl:* Late 18th-century Claude Glass, Science Museum, London. **pp46–47:** *Landscape with the Marriage of Isaac and Rebekah ("The Mill")*, Claude, NGL. **p47:** *tr: Drawing – Landscape with St. John the Baptist and Angels*, Claude, The Trustees of the British Museum, London

Pages 48–49 Composing with light
p48: *tl: Photograph of Rouen Cathedral*, © Roger-Viollet; *bl: Rouen Cathedral: Effects of the Sun, End of the Day*, Claude Monet, MM; *bc: Rouen Cathedral: The Portal and the Tower of Saint Romain, Morning Effect, Harmony in White*, MM; *br: Rouen Cathedral: Full Sunlight, Harmony in Blue and Gold*, Monet, MM. **pp48–49:** Sketch books (Rouen), Monet, MM. **p49:** *t: Snowstorm: Steamboat off a Harbour's*

Continued on p. 64

Index

Mouth, J. M. W. Turner, TG/AKG; *bl: Rouen Cathedral: Morning Sun, Harmony in Blue*, Monet, MM; *bc: Rouen Cathedral: The Portal, Grey Weather*, Monet, MM; *br: Rouen Cathedral: The Portal Seen From the Front, Harmony in Brown*, Monet, MM

Pages 50–51 Pure colour
p50: *t: IKB 79*, Yves Klein, TG/© ADAGP, Paris and DACS, London 1995; *b: Rain*, Howard Hodgkin, TG. **p51:** *t: Portrait of Mme Matisse, the Green Stripe*, Henri Matisse, Statens Museum for Kunst, Copenhagen/© Succession H. Matisse/DACS 1995

Pages 52–53 Using photography
p52: *cl:* Degas-type camera (Portable 9-12), Gilles-Falere, Musée Français de la Photographie, Bièvres (Fondé et Animé depuis 1960 par Jean et André Fage); *b: Le Boulevard Montmartre: Rainy Weather, Afternoon*, Camille Pissarro, Christie's, London/Bridgeman Art Library. **pp52–53:** *tr: Bld. de Strasbourg* (Stereoscopic photograph), Hippolyte Jouvin, Collection André Jamme, Paris. **p53:** *tr: La La at the Cirque Fernando, Paris*, Edgar Degas, NGL; *bl: Dancers in the Wings*, Degas, The Norton Simon Art Foundation, M.1977.6.P.; *br: Snapshot*, Degas, Bibliothèque Nationale, Paris

Pages 54–55 Depicting motion
p54: *bl: Napoleon Crossing the Alps*, Jacques Louis David, Schloss Charlottenburg, Berlin/Bridgeman Art Library; *cr: Swifts: Paths of Movement and Dynamic Sequences*, Giacomo Balla, The Museum of Modern Art, New York. Purchase.; **pp54–55:** *Chronophotograph of Flight of a Bird*, Etienne Jules Marey/Archives de Cinemathèque Française. **p55:** *r: Nude Descending a Staircase, No. 2*, Marcel Duchamp, Philadelphia Museum of Art/AKG/© ADAGP, Paris and DACS, London 1995; *bl: Chronophotograph of Figure during Standing Jump*, Marey or follower

Pages 56–57 Double images
p56: *br: Water*, Giuseppe Arcimboldo, KHM. **pp56–57:** *Metamorphosis of Narcissus*, Salvador Dali, TG/© DEMART PRO ARTE BV/DACS 1995. **p57:** *bl: Da-Dandy*, Hannah Höch, Private Collection/Visual Arts Library/© DACS 1995; *tr: Photo of Salvador Dali*, Dept. Stills, Posters and Designs, British Film Institute, London

Pages 58–59 The role of chance
p58: *l: The Way Out at Last*, Paul Klee, Private Collection, Switzerland/Kunstmuseum, Bern/© DACS 1995. **pp58-59:** *View of the Port of St. Denis*, Max Ernst, OKB/Hans Hinz – Artothek/© SPADEM/ADAGP, Paris and DACS, London 1995

Pages 60-61 Breaking the frame
p60: *cl: Still Life*, Pablo Picasso, TG/© DACS 1995. **pp60–61:** *c: Déjeuner sur le Plancher*, Julian Opie, Courtesy Lisson Gallery, London. **p61:** *tr, cr: Steller's Albatross (#6, 5.5X)*, Frank Stella, Private Collection, San Francisco/© Frank Stella/Artists Rights Society, New York

Pages 62-63 Glossary
p62: *tl: Landscape with the Marriage of Isaac and Rebekah ("The Mill")*, Claude, NGL; *tr: The Street Singer*, Edouard Manet, Bequest of Sarah Choate Sears in memory of her husband, Joshua Montgomery Sears, courtesy of Museum of Fine Arts, Boston; *bl: The Baptism of Christ*, Piero della Francesca, NGL; *br: The Night Watch*, Rembrandt van Rijn, Rijksmuseum, Amsterdam. **p63:** *l: Madonna della Sedia*, Raphael, Galleria Palatina, Florence/SC; *r: Horse Attacked by a Lion*, George Stubbs, TG

Acknowledgements

Key: *t:* top; *b:* bottom; *c:* centre; *l:* left; *r:* right

Photography for Dorling Kindersley:
Andreas von Einsiedal: fc: *tl*; p3: *tl*; p32: *tl*
Alison Harris: p4: *top*; p52: *cl*
Susannah Price: p31; p49: *b,c*; p51: *b*
Philippe Sebert: p7: *b*; p12: *b*; p35: *tr*
Artworks:
John Woodcock: p14:*br*; p15:*cr*; p33:*br*

Dorling Kindersley would like to thank:
Gillian Burtwell and Lisa Harris at the National Gallery, London; A.P. Fitzpatrick Art Materials; Anthony d'Offay Gallery, London; Collection André Jamme, Paris; Dave "Big Wave" Walton for his thorough editorial assistance; and Hilary Bird for a superbly compiled index.

Author's acknowledgements:
My thanks go to the following members of the Eyewitness Art team: Mark Johnson Davies who has brought these pages to life with his imaginative design; Phil Hunt, my editor, who has meticulously checked details and kept open a weather eye for howlers of various kinds; Sean Moore, who invited me to write the book and whose support and encouragement has been vital; Gwen Edmonds for her invaluable suggestions; and Helen Castle for her helpful observations and research.